THE
COMPLETE
IDIOT'S
GUIDE TO

Spices and Herbs

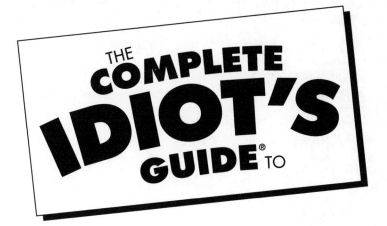

THE COMPLETE IDIOT'S GUIDE® TO

Spices and Herbs

by Leslie Bilderback, CMB

ALPHA

A member of Penguin Group (USA) Inc.

ALPHA BOOKS

Published by the Penguin Group

Penguin Group (USA) Inc., 375 Hudson Street, New York, New York 10014, USA

Penguin Group (Canada), 90 Eglinton Avenue East, Suite 700, Toronto, Ontario M4P 2Y3, Canada (a division of Pearson Penguin Canada Inc.)

Penguin Books Ltd., 80 Strand, London WC2R 0RL, England

Penguin Ireland, 25 St. Stephen's Green, Dublin 2, Ireland (a division of Penguin Books Ltd.)

Penguin Group (Australia), 250 Camberwell Road, Camberwell, Victoria 3124, Australia (a division of Pearson Australia Group Pty. Ltd.)

Penguin Books India Pvt. Ltd., 11 Community Centre, Panchsheel Park, New Delhi—110 017, India

Penguin Group (NZ), 67 Apollo Drive, Rosedale, North Shore, Auckland 1311, New Zealand (a division of Pearson New Zealand Ltd.)

Penguin Books (South Africa) (Pty.) Ltd., 24 Sturdee Avenue, Rosebank, Johannesburg 2196, South Africa

Penguin Books Ltd., Registered Offices: 80 Strand, London WC2R 0RL, England

International Standard Book Number: 978-1-59257-674-6
Library of Congress Catalog Card Number: 2007930853

09   08   07   8   7   6   5   4   3   2   1

Interpretation of the printing code: The rightmost number of the first series of numbers is the year of the book's printing; the rightmost number of the second series of numbers is the number of the book's printing. For example, a printing code of 07-1 shows that the first printing occurred in 2007.

Printed in the United States of America

Note: This publication contains the opinions and ideas of its author. It is intended to provide helpful and informative material on the subject matter covered. It is sold with the understanding that the author and publisher are not engaged in rendering professional services in the book. If the reader requires personal assistance or advice, a competent professional should be consulted.

The author and publisher specifically disclaim any responsibility for any liability, loss, or risk, personal or otherwise, which is incurred as a consequence, directly or indirectly, of the use and application of any of the contents of this book.

Most Alpha books are available at special quantity discounts for bulk purchases for sales promotions, premiums, fund-raising, or educational use. Special books, or book excerpts, can also be created to fit specific needs.

For details, write: Special Markets, Alpha Books, 375 Hudson Street, New York, NY 10014.

Publisher: *Marie Butler-Knight*
Editorial Director: *Mike Sanders*
Managing Editor: *Billy Fields*
Senior Acquisitions Editor: *Paul Dinas*
Senior Development Editor: *Christy Wagner*
Production Editor: *Megan Douglass*

Copy Editor: *Jan Zoya*
Cartoonist: *Shannon Wheeler*
Cover Designer: *Kurt Owens*
Book Designer: *Becky Harmon*
Layout: *Ayanna Lacey*
Proofreader: *Mary Hunt*

Contents at a Glance

Contents

Appendixes

C Chile Pepper Guide 247

Introduction

Do you every wander down the herb and spice aisle at your grocery store and wonder what people do with all those powders and seeds? When you dine out, do you ever wonder what makes a particular dish taste the way it does? If so, you're in luck! This book unlocks those mysteries and emboldens you to experiment with spices, herbs, tastes, and flavors like you never have before.

Spices and herbs have an ancient and honorable history. The search for, and marketing of, spices has been creating wealth for centuries. Spices were so valuable that in ancient Egypt, Greece, and Rome, they were used as currency. Herbs were also coveted for their medicinal and magical properties. Many of these ancient remedies are still in use today. But more than an interesting past, spices and herbs have changed eating from simply providing sustenance into an art form. Seasoning is no longer for preservation or palatability. It is done for fun.

Modern cookery has not only advanced technologically, but culinarily as well. And thanks to television and the Internet, even if you live in the middle of nowhere, your neighborhood is global. Within a 5-mile radius of my house (not counting fast food), I have several Mexican restaurants, 2 barbecue restaurants, 2 Thai restaurants, an Indian restaurant, 3 Chinese restaurants, 2 Japanese restaurants, 2 Italian restaurants, a Jamaican restaurant, and a classic French restaurant. Each of these establishments serves chicken, but thanks to spices and herbs, not one is the same. They are defined by the seasonings, the cuisine, the culture, and the chef.

The cuisine of a particular country is first defined by the regional availability of foods and the way people utilized what they had on hand to fulfill their basic nutritional needs. For instance, corn, beans, and chiles are native to Central and South America, and so these foods are utilized in many of their regional specialties. Coastal civilizations utilize the bounty of the sea. Inland people learned to hunt. Agriculture took hold, and people learned to grow what they needed. As civilizations progressed, and basic needs were met, taste gained importance. Spices and herbs, fruits, and vegetables were gathered or cultivated and used to add interest to food.

As people began to wander, they shared ingredients and insights, introducing new foods and flavors to each other. Chiles from the New World ended up in Europe and became a vital element in the cuisines of Hungary and Spain. Citrus moved from Asia to Europe, to the New World, where it thrived. Melons, yams, and sesame came from Africa to the New World with the slaves and became an integral part of the American culture.

Consequently, we have developed a global palate. Demand has increased for foods from far-off lands. We want to learn how to cook like the peasants of Germany and Argentina and Morocco. We want to eat like the kings of Russia and Persia and Siam. Thankfully, we can. Extravagant ingredients aren't all that extravagant anymore, and they are relatively easy to come by. Through the Internet, and a global market that brings the weird and wonderful foods of the world to our local markets, we can experience the wonders of international cuisine in the comfort of our own homes.

How to Use This Book

This book is divided into two parts. In **Part 1, "The Spice of Life,"** you learn how to buy spices and herbs at their freshest, how to store them, and how to use them to their best advantage. And if you're interested in the freshest possible ingredients, you'll learn how to grow spices and herbs yourself, in the backyard or on the windowsill. There are recipes, too, for flavoring vinegars, oils, butters, and even potpourri, all designed to preserve the flavor and aroma of spices and herbs.

This first section also delves into the how and why of taste and flavor. It discusses the basic elements of taste and how they combine to give each food its unique qualities.

In **Part 2, "Flavor at Your Fingertips,"** you'll find an exhaustive list of all the common, and many not-so-common, spices and herbs. It explains what they look like, taste like, and how they are used. It also provides sources for the more unusual, hard-to-get entries. Scattered throughout the list are a few ingredients that do not fall into the category of spice or herb, such as baking soda. But because it's found on the same shelf in your market (and your pantry), I've included it.

Recipes are sprinkled throughout the list as well—beverages, soups, meat dishes, snacks, and desserts, all designed to whet your appetite for the new and different. The recipes illustrate how the spice or herb is classically used, or give some ideas for more unusual ways to use the flavor.

The appendixes contain recipes for spice and herb blends. Some are interpretations of commonly available mixes, like Italian Herbs or Cajun Spice. Others are exotic blends from far-off lands. You'll also find information on the form and function of fresh and dried chiles, including their heat levels.

Extras

Throughout the book you'll see sidebars sprinkled here and there. They provide just a little more information you might find useful.

Tidbit

These sidebars include tips and general notes about a spice or an herb.

Chefspeak

These boxes explain culinary-specific terminology you might not be familiar with.

Hot Stuff

"Hot stuff!" is a classic warning in professional kitchens. What better name for these warning boxes that alert you to potential problems or hazards.

Acknowledgments

Thanks to Paul Dinas for thinking of me for this project. You have reawakened my desire to travel afar and taste the world. Thanks, as always, to my supportive family, Bill, Emma, and Claire, who take extra good care of me when I've had too much curry. (Is there ever too much, really?) Thanks to Mom, for teaching me that one should never be without cardamom.

Trademarks

All terms mentioned in this book that are known to be or are suspected of being trademarks or service marks have been appropriately capitalized. Alpha Books and Penguin Group (USA) Inc. cannot attest to the accuracy of this information. Use of a term in this book should not be regarded as affecting the validity of any trademark or service mark.

The Spice of Life

Spices make the world go 'round. At least they did 500 years ago. It was for want of spice that the great Portuguese mariners set out on quests for riches. They spread their spice lust throughout Europe, and a New World was discovered.

Why did flavor carry so much influence, and how does it influence us today? Why do we crave something sweet at one time and something salty another? Why does one person love a flavor, while another avoids it like the plague? And what makes one flavor complement another? These mysteries of taste will unravel before you in the following chapters.

In Part 1, you learn how to choose and use herbs and spices to their best advantage, in traditional ways as well as recipes and food pairings you might not have considered. You'll also learn how to grow them for yourself, and what to do with your first bumper crop.

Chapter 1

Using Spices and Herbs

In This Chapter

◆ Understanding the influence spices and herbs have had on civilization

◆ How to best buy, use, and store spices and herbs

◆ The mystique of spices and herbs

◆ Spice and herb flavor compatibility

Some might see them as simply the contents of little jars in our kitchen cabinets we pull out from time to time when we're feeling culinarily creative. But throughout human history, spices and herbs have meant much more. For centuries, spices and herbs have defined cultures and ethnic diversity. They displayed wealth and civic pride. They were the impetus of modern trade, the rationale behind decisions of settlement, and reasons for the discovery of new worlds.

A Brief History

Today, as throughout history, herbs are used for their fragrance, flavor, color, and medicinal properties. Five thousand years ago, the Sumerians documented medicinal uses of a few herbs. Four thousand years ago, the Chinese used more than 300 herbs for their healing properties. Three thousand years ago, the Egyptians expanded use from the merely pharmaceutical (including mummification) to culinary and cosmetic use. The Greeks used herbs to adorn the heads of their heroes, and the ancient Romans used herbs for magic and sorcery. The Old Testament includes much about herbs, and the Middle Ages saw herb cultivation, with studies revolving around the monasteries. Superstitions surrounded herbs well into the eighteenth and nineteenth centuries, until modern chemistry and the study of the physical sciences began to advance.

In the ancient world, herbs were largely medicinal and spiritual and were grown or gathered easily. Spices were a luxury item and, consequently, one of the world's most valuable trade goods. They were light and didn't require special preservation like other foods. That, combined with their multiple uses, made spices a hot commodity. And while we still use spices for dyes, medicines, and cosmetics, their most beloved characteristic is their flavor.

Tidbit

It's long been thought that the use of spices and herbs in cookery began out of necessity. If large animals were not consumed soon after a kill, the meat had to be preserved. With no refrigeration, poorly preserved meat began to rot. It was once thought that spices were used to mask foul flavors and increase palatability. However, most scholars today agree that spices were luxury items, and those who could afford them could certainly also afford fresh meat.

While black pepper appears profusely in the fifth century C.E. Roman cookbook *De re Coquinaria* (*On the Subject of Cooking*, commonly known as *Apicius*), the spice trade didn't really begin in earnest until the third century, when trade from Malaysia to China began. Alexander the Great began exchanging rice and cotton for spices to please the Greeks.

The Muslims controlled the overland spice route from approximately 700 to 1000 C.E. Crusaders passing through brought the desire for spices home to Europe.

During the Middle Ages, cinnamon, clove, nutmeg, and pepper were most prized by medieval traders. In the late fourteenth and early fifteenth centuries, the Spanish and Portuguese began searching for ways to get in on the spice-trade action. Thus began the age of exploration. While looking for a trade route, Marco Polo found China, Christopher Columbus found the New World, and Ferdinand Magellan circumnavigated the globe. All this, spurred on by the love of spice and the promise of wealth.

Spices

Spices are the bark, seed, resin, root, stem, fruit, or bud of a plant, tree, or shrub. They count amongst their rank the familiar, such as *cinnamon, mustard, ginger, licorice, juniper,* and *cloves.* Also included are the strange and exotic, including *asafetida, nigella, silphium,* and *grains of paradise.* Many can be found at your neighborhood market, and some can only be obtained on the other side of the globe.

In the ancient world, spice merchants held all the cards. Middlemen of Phoenicia (modern Syria and Lebanon), Cairo, Alexandria, Venice, and Genoa befriended pharaoh's and kings in an attempt to monopolize the lucrative spice market. In a time when a human being could be traded for a handful of pepper, you can bet it was a competitive business. Before the age of exploration, spice sources were closely held secrets.

Spices spread more than flavor and wealth. The prophet Mohammed used spice trade as a platform from which to spread his message, capturing attention with his spices and then captivating with his words. And three kings are said to have traveled to Bethlehem bearing at least two spices, *frankincense* and *myrrh.*

Tidbit

Early records give us a glimpse into the practice, ethical or not, of cutting spices with sawdust, dirt, and rocks. They also show penalties for such behavior, which often included a toasty death.

Cooking With Spices

Spices are available whole and ground. They begin to lose their flavor and aroma as soon as they are ground, and the longer they sit on the shelf, the weaker they get. The most economical and flavorful way to purchase spice is in whole form. Spices kept whole will last for years with little loss of flavor and can be ground as needed.

Hot Stuff

If you're going to use a coffee grinder, consider keeping a separate grinder for your spices. Otherwise, your coffee will start tasting weird.

In centuries past, a *mortar* was used to grind whole spices. A classic chef's method called *mignonette* uses a sauté pan to rub and crush whole spices against a cutting board. There are special spice graters and grinders at every gourmet gadget shop. But perhaps the easiest way to grind spices today is with a coffee grinder.

Some spices, especially seeds, benefit from light toasting prior to grinding to help release their aromatic oils. You can do this in a dry sauté pan on top of the stove. Keep the spices moving as they heat up, and remove them from the heat, and the hot pan, as soon as you smell the spice. Let the toasted spices cool down for a few minutes before you grind them.

Chefspeak

A **mortar** is a bowl, usually made of ceramic or stone, into which spices, herbs, vegetables, or pharmaceuticals are put to be crushed by a *pestle*, a hard instrument shaped like a small baseball bat. **Macerate** means to soak food, usually fruit, in liquid to infuse flavor.

Other spices such as *annatto* or *saffron* should be heated in oil or other liquid to release and trap their essence. Others, like mustard, don't have much flavor at all until they're moistened and allowed to *macerate*.

Larger spices, like *nutmeg* and *cinnamon*, can be broken into smaller pieces before being ground. A meat mallet is a perfect tool for this. If you're into gadgets, you can buy special graters designed especially for large spices.

More Bang for Your Spice Buck

Smaller ethnic markets usually have the best spice prices. Buy them in tiny cellophane packages and empty them into clean, airtight jars when you get home. Store spices in a cool, dark, dry place to prolong their flavor. You can also find many online sources for whole and ground spices and spice blends. In Part 2, I suggest online sources for many of the spices and herbs listed.

To get their maximum effect in your recipes, add spices early in the cooking process. Because fat is a natural flavor carrier, adding your spices to oil or butter brings out the flavors and permeates a recipe.

Herbs

Herbs are green, leafy plants. With a few exceptions (such as *bay* and *rosemary*), they have delicate, nonwoody stems. If allowed to grow to maturity, herbs develop into flowers and seeds. Many of these seeds are then reclassified as spices when dried.

You can purchase herbs in fresh or dried forms, and although they can be substituted for one another, the two forms have very different characteristics that are worth noting.

Dried Herbs

When herbs are dried, the water in the leaves evaporates and the oils intensify, which is why dried herbs tend to have stronger flavor than their fresh counterparts. However, dried herbs lose their flavor very quickly. Ground and powdered herbs have an increased surface area that allows the oils to dissipate faster.

Buy dried herbs in small quantities, rather than in large life-time supply–size containers. Store them in a cool, dry, dark space to maximize their lifespan. To release more of the dried herb oil, rub it in your hands before adding it to a recipe. Dried herbs that are powdered tend to be stronger than those that are granulated, crushed, or crumbled.

Hot Stuff

If you can't smell your dried herbs after rubbing them in your hand, replace them.

Cooking dried herbs for prolonged periods diminishes their flavor. Add dried herbs in the last 30 minutes of a recipe for maximum effect. In cold recipes, like salads and marinades, the longer the herb is in contact with the food, the more intense the flavor will be. In baking, incorporate herbs with the fat in the recipe for more even distribution throughout the batter or dough.

Fresh Herbs

When gathering fresh herbs (in the grocery store or the garden), look for bright green leaves that stay on the stem. You shouldn't see any bruised or dried leaves, and the stems should be straight and firm. Limp, dry, bruised, or sad-looking herbs are rarely worth the price you pay.

Tidbit

Fresh herbs can be costly in supermarkets, so look for better deals at farmers' markets and neighborhood ethnic grocers. Most large markets sell a couple stems of herbs carefully sealed and beautifully packaged. But purveyors who cater to a specific culture buy the most sought-after herbs in much larger quantities and sell them cheaper. Within 4 miles of my house, one store sells cilantro for $2.49 a bunch, while another sells 3 bunches for 99 cents. Guess where I shop.

It's easy to waste fresh herbs unless you know how to store them and how to utilize the leftovers. When the fresh herbs come home, wash them right away—thoroughly, but gently. I like to submerge them in water for a minute to be sure all the sand, soil, and bugs are removed. Shake them dry and let them drain in a colander for a few minutes before refrigerating.

There are several excellent ways to store fresh herbs in the fridge. A good rule is to think of your herbs as fresh flowers. You can stand them upright in a glass of water and loosely cover the top with a plastic bag to keep the moisture in. You can also wrap the washed herbs loosely in paper towels and store them in the produce drawer. As a professional chef, I used to hang my herbs from a clothesline rigged up in the back of the walk-in refrigerator, loosely wrapped in plastic bags. Use any method that will keep them from getting smashed.

When adding fresh herbs into recipes, keep in mind that you need more fresh herbs than dried. A general conversion rule is 3 parts fresh herb to 1 part dry. Chopping them very fine—such as in a *chiffonade* or *julienne*—exposes as much surface area as possible, which in turn allows the most flavor to be released. When garnishing with sprigs of herbs, remember that they contain a lot of water and will wilt if they get hot and dry. And like any green vegetable, herbs discolor if overcooked. Add them into recipes at the very end of cooking to maximize flavor and appearance.

Leftover herbs are easily stored for later use. Freeze chopped herbs in plastic bags, or mix them with water and freeze them in an ice cube tray. You can dry them yourself in the microwave between paper towels, or preserve their flavor in oils, vinegars, and compound butters.

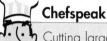

Chefspeak

Cutting large-leafed herbs into strips is called a **chiffonade**. You do it by stacking the leaves, rolling them into a log, and slicing off coin shapes, which uncoil into **julienne** strips.

Tidbit

Herbs are easily cultivated from seeds or plants in a garden, indoors or out. See Chapter 2 for instructions on growing and preserving spices and herbs.

Ancient Remedies and Power

Herb gardening and cultivation is an ancient tradition. Egyptians, Greeks, and Romans, kept herbs close at hand, growing them in ornamental courtyards, pots, and public areas. In the ninth century, Emperor Charlemagne regulated agriculture, detailing 73 herbs to be planted in gardens at each of his estates throughout the Empire. In the 1500s, gardens filled with medicinal herbs were planted throughout Europe. Called *physic gardens,* they were planted specifically by and for apothecaries.

There's no question that spices and herbs played a major role in the history of medicine. Due, perhaps, to their seemingly magical powers of altering the physical state, they took on mystical significance as well. The following list gives a glimpse into the flavorful folklore of the more common spices and herbs.

Allspice   Caribbean folk medicine included the use of allspice to cure colds, cramps, and upset stomach, and the Mayans included it in their embalming ritual. Once introduced to Europe, allspice was believed to bring about good luck and financial prosperity.

Basil   Native to Africa and India, basil was probably brought from India to Greece by early trade of Alexander the Great. It's a sacred plant in India, associated with the Hindu goddess Tulasi, and remains a symbol of love, faithfulness, and eternal life. Basil is a symbol of love in Italy and Eastern Europe, thought to be an aphrodisiac and a love potion. The name Basil comes from the Greek *basileus*, which means "king." In France, the herb is still known as *herbe royale*.

Basil is also associated with the scorpion, thought to protect against them in some cultures, and attract them in others. In England, it was used to ward off evil spirits and insects. Christians believe basil grew at the sight of the cross, which is why it's found on the altar and in the Holy Water at the Greek Orthodox Church.

Coriander   One of the first herbs grown by the colonists in the New World, coriander is said to relieve abdominal pain. The Chinese associated it with immortality, and the in the Middle Ages, it was commonly used as an aphrodisiac.

Cumin   Cumin was used as a bit of marital insurance, carried in ceremonies to ensure happiness and used to keep lovers from straying. It was also used as a remedy for the common cold.

Dill   The Greeks saw dill as a sign of wealth. It was used to aid digestion and calm the nerves. Europeans hung it about the home and made it into potions as protection against witchcraft. Bathing in water infused with dill was said to make you irresistible to your lover.

Fennel   The ancient Greek named this herb Marathon, after the battle that took place in a field of fennel. The Romans chewed fennel as an appetite suppressant, and puritans chewed it during fasting to keep hunger at bay. Fennel was hung throughout medieval homes for luck and to keep away ghosts.

Marjoram   Ancient Greeks set their sheep and goats to graze on hillsides of marjoram, believing it made the meat tender and delicious. A favorite herb of Aphrodite, marjoram was once believed to induce dreams of one's future mate. As a symbol of love and happiness, marjoram wreaths crowned the wedding couple and adorned gravesites. Hippocrates used it as an antiseptic, and the Egyptians used it as a disinfectant. In the Middle Ages, it was chewed to relieve toothaches and indigestion.

Mint   Minthe is the name of Hades' lover. In retaliation, she was turned into a low-growing herb by his wife Persephone, destined to be stepped upon for all eternity. Despite this mythology, mint has been considered a symbol of hospitality since Roman times. The Greeks believed that mint stirred up bodily lust, and soldiers were warned to stay away from it, lest they lose courage and strength from increased lovemaking.

Parsley   This herb has been used to anoint champions, celebrate spring, and curse enemies. The natural ability of chlorophyll to absorb foul odor was put to good use in the Middle Ages, when parsley was strewn about tables and people. Its absorption potential was also employed as an antidote to poison and as hangover prevention.

Rosemary   The Greeks believed rosemary improved their memory. Students carried it to examinations, and lovers used it to ensure fidelity. The smoke of burning rosemary was used to ward off sickness and evil demons, and the herb was hung around the home for protection and luck. Unmarried women believed the name of their future husband would come to them during sleep if they placed rosemary under their pillow.

It's said that Mary placed her blue cloak atop a rosemary bush, changing its white flowers to blue. Still more Christian association says the rosemary shrub will never grow taller than Christ's height and never live longer than 33 years.

Sage   The ancient Greeks, Romans, and Arabs all believed sage to induce immortality and wisdom. Thus, it was used to treat memory loss and a host of illnesses, including fever and stomach disorders. It symbolized domestic virtue and skill, and as such, a house with a garden overflowing with sage was said to contain a strong-willed woman.

Tarragon   The name, derived from the French *esdragon*, meaning "little dragon," is a reference to its serpentine root system, which led medieval healers to use it as a remedy for snake bites. The ancient Greeks used tarragon as a cure for toothaches, and it was considered a calming herb. Also referred to as a *banishing herb*, tarragon was used as incense while the name of one's nemesis was written on a piece of paper and then burned.

Thyme   Native to Southern Europe and the Mediterranean, thyme has long been associated with courage. Ancient Egyptians used it in embalming, and the ancient Greeks believed it would make them brave. They burnt it as incense, bathed in it, and used it as treatment for shyness and depression. In the Middle Ages, thyme was given to knights to encourage bravery and hidden under pillows to ward off nightmares. Shakespeare wrote of the fairy queen, Tatiana, who slept in a bed of wild thyme, and English folklore includes recipes using thyme designed to lure fairies out into the open.

Cooking Creatively with Spices and Herbs

After reading about spices and herbs, you're probably itching to taste some. (Throughout the writing of this book, I have experienced several severe cravings for Indian food.) Before you go pair the first spice or herb you find with the first dish of food placed in front of you, a little more reading first. The following list includes the most common spices and herbs and, in general, the types of foods they're compatible with:

Allspice   Apples, beets, cabbage, caramel, cardamom, cinnamon, foie gras, game meats, ginger, juniper, nuts, nutmeg, onions, pears, poultry, pumpkin, root vegetables, seafood

Anise   Apples, beets, beef, caramel, carrots, chocolate, citrus, cinnamon, coconut, cranberry, figs, foie gras, game meats, root vegetables, seafood, stone fruits, tea

Basil   Artichokes, beef, blue cheese, coconut, eggplant, figs, garlic, leafy vegetables, mint, mushrooms, olives, oregano, parsley, peaches, poultry, raspberries, rosemary, seafood, thyme, tomato, vinegar

Bay   Artichokes, apples, bananas, beans, beef, blue cheese, citrus, dates, figs, game meats, grains, mushrooms, nuts, potatoes, poultry, seafood, stone fruits, tamarind, thyme, tomatoes

Caraway   Beets, cabbage, cheese, cured meats, dill, fennel, garlic, nuts, mushrooms, onions, oregano, potatoes, root vegetables, sausage, seafood, yeast breads

Cardamom   Apples, bananas, beans, caramel, cinnamon, citrus, coconut, coffee, coriander, curry, dates, ginger, grains, grains of paradise, nuts, pepper, pumpkin, sugar, squash, yeast breads

Chervil   Artichokes, asparagus, carrots, cheese, chives, citrus, eggs, grains, green beans, leafy vegetables, mushrooms, nuts, onions, parsley, pasta, potatoes, seafood, tarragon, thyme, vinegar

Chiles   Bananas, beans, cheese, cilantro, cinnamon, citrus, chocolate, coconut, corn, cumin, basil, beef, garlic, ginger, grains, oregano, potatoes, poultry, seafood, tropical fruits

Chives   Asparagus, beets, blue cheese, chervil, dill, eggs, horseradish, leafy greens, mushrooms, olives, pasta, parsley, potatoes, seafood, tarragon

Cilantro   Avocados, beef, chiles, citrus, coconut, coriander, corn, cumin, curry, dates, fennel, figs, garlic, mint, oregano, pepper, sausage, seafood, tomatoes, yogurt

Cinnamon   Allspice, apples, bananas, beans, caramel, cardamom, chiles, chocolate, clove, coffee, cranberry, curry, dates, game meats, figs, foie gras, ginger, grains, nutmeg, pumpkin, stone fruit, sugar, squash, tea, vanilla

Clove   Apples, beets, cinnamon, citrus, foie gras, game meats, ginger, grains of paradise, nuts, nutmeg, peaches, pineapple, pumpkin, root vegetables, sausages, stone fruit, tomatoes, vanilla

Coriander   Bananas, beans, cilantro, cumin, cured meats, curry, game meats, mint, parsley, poultry, root vegetables, seafood, tomatoes

Cumin   Avocados, beans, beef, cilantro, citrus, coconut, cucumber, garlic, grains, mango, mint, onion, parsley, poultry, sausages, seafood, tomatoes

Dill   Anise, beets, blue cheese, cabbage, caraway, carrots, chives, cucumbers, eggs, fennel, mint, oregano, parsley, potatoes, seafood, tarragon, tomatoes, veal, yeast bread

Fennel   Artichokes, anise, apples, artichokes, basil, beans, blue cheese, cabbage, cilantro, dill, eggplant, figs, garlic, olives, onions, oregano, parsley, potatoes, thyme, tomato, sausage, seafood, veal

Fenugreek   Allspice, beans, cumin, cardamom, chiles, cinnamon, curry, game meats, ginger, potatoes, poultry

Ginger   Allspice, anise, asparagus, bananas, carrots, chiles, chives, chocolate, cinnamon, citrus, cloves, coconut, coriander, cranberry, cumin, curry, dates, fennel, figs, garlic, jasmine, nutmeg, onions, pears, pepper, poultry, pumpkin, raisins, root vegetables, rose, seafood, stone fruits, sugar, tea, tropical fruits

Horseradish   Apples, beef, beets, blue cheese, capers, chives, citrus, cured meats, dill, nuts, mustard, onions, potatoes, sausage, seafood, root vegetables, vinegar

Juniper   Allspice, beef, blue cheese, cabbage, cilantro, cured meats, game meats, garlic, lavender, olives, oregano, pepper, poultry, rosemary, veal, vinegar

Lavender   Anise, apples, berries, cranberry, fennel, figs, foie gras, game meats, garlic, juniper, rose, rosemary, thyme, olives, oregano, potato, sage, stone fruit, sugar, tarragon, tea

Lemongrass   Berries, carrots, chiles, cilantro, coriander, coconut, curry, garlic, onions, pepper, poultry, parsley, seafood, tea, thyme, tomato

Mint   Basil, beans, beef, carrots, chocolate, cilantro, citrus, coconut, coriander, cranberry, eggplant, fennel, figs, game meats, garlic, grains, parsley, poultry, seafood, tea, yogurt

Mustard   Anchovy, anise, asparagus, beef, beets, blue cheese, cabbage, capers, chiles, cured meats, fennel, honey, poultry, root vegetables, sausage, seafood, vinegar, yeast bread

Nutmeg   Allspice, asparagus, blue cheese, cabbage, carrots, cinnamon, cheese, clove, coffee, cranberries, cumin, eggs, foie gras, ginger, green beans, pasta, peaches, pumpkin, potato, sausage, sugar, vanilla, veal

Oregano   Artichokes, basil, beans, beef, blue cheese, cinnamon, cumin, eggplant, fennel, garlic, mushrooms, nuts, parsley, pasta, poultry, seafood, squash, thyme, tomatoes, veal

Parsley   Artichokes, asparagus, basil, bay, beans, beef, chervil, chives, dill, game meats, garlic, mushrooms, grains, onions, oregano, pasta, potatoes, poultry, seafood, thyme, tomatoes

Pepper   Allspice, artichokes, asparagus, beef, blue cheese, cheese, cinnamon, citrus, eggs, figs, foie gras, game meats, ginger, mushrooms, pineapple, poultry, seafood, sugar, tomatoes

Rosemary   Apples, asparagus, basil, beans, beef, blue cheese, caramel, citrus, cranberry, game meats, garlic, grains, fennel, figs, mushrooms, nuts, onion, oregano, parsley, potatoes, poultry, raisins, sage, seafood, sugar, thyme, tomatoes

Saffron   Basil, bay, berries, chives, cinnamon, cloves, coriander, cumin, curry, fennel, garlic, ginger, grains, mint, parsley, poultry, sausage, seafood, tomatoes

Sage   Anchovy, capers, citrus, cranberry, beef, blue cheese, game meats, garlic, green beans, lavender, mushrooms, nuts, parsley, plums, poultry, rosemary, seafood, thyme, veal

Sesame   Bananas, beans, cinnamon, citrus, coconut, eggplant, game meats, garlic, ginger, leafy greens, nuts, mustard, onions, pasta, pepper, poultry, root vegetables, rosemary, seafood, stone fruits, thyme, vinegar, yeast bread

Sorrel   Chives, beans, beef, blue cheese, eggs, leafy greens, oregano, parsley, poultry, thyme, seafood, squash

Tarragon   Artichokes, carrots, chervil, citrus, eggs, foie gras, garlic, leafy greens, mushrooms, onion, oregano, parsley, potatoes, poultry, seafood, thyme, tomatoes, veal

Thyme   Artichokes, bananas, basil, bay, beans, blue cheese, carrots, chervil, citrus, cranberry, dates, dill, figs, mint, mushrooms, nuts, onion, oregano, parsley, potatoes, poultry, raisins, sage, seafood, stone fruit, tomatoes

Vanilla   Apples, bananas, caramel, chocolate, chiles, cinnamon, citrus, coconut, coffee, dates, figs, lavender, nuts, shell fish, stone fruit, tropical fruit

The list is a compilation of common and unique flavor combinations gathered from regional and international cuisine, as well as a 20-year career of cooking with creative, innovative chefs. Some will seem obvious, such as basil and garlic. Others you might find a little more out-there. I urge you to give those more unusual combinations some thought, and perhaps a try. They are listed because they work together, each flavor bringing out interesting qualities of the other.

The list is not nearly as complete as the encyclopedic bulk of this book (Part 2) because many of the herbs and spices carry similar flavor characteristics. For instance, marjoram is very similar to oregano and could be paired with the same foods that appear on the *oregano* list. Similarly, lemon verbena, lemon balm, lemon myrtle, and lemons could all pair with the foods on the *lemongrass* list. Use the list as a guideline for experimentation with all the entries in this book.

> **Tidbit**
>
> Some of these parings work better than others. The more you cook, the more you will develop your own preferences for food pairings.

The foods on the list are generalized. For instance, poultry could be chicken, duck, turkey, quail, or ostrich. Citrus includes lemons, limes, oranges, and the like. Grains could be rice, oatmeal, or quinoa. Of course, those foods do not all taste the same, but they all combine favorably with the title flavor.

There are also foods that do not appear on the list. For instance, pork is not here, because it will usually work with the flavors that complement poultry. Rhubarb isn't here, but foods with a similar effect—like citrus, cranberries, tamarind, and tropical fruits—are. Experiment accordingly.

Finally, the list is not meant to be recipes. The foods that appear on a given list won't necessarily all work together. The title herb or spice enhances each food, individually. In some cases you can make combinations, but that is up to you, the cook, to experiment with. If you doubt the compatibility of foods on the list, test them before you commit to a full-blown recipe. Gather a small quantity of the foods, and taste them together. Try them in different proportions, and add some of the basic taste elements, like salt, sugar, or acid. Rinse your mouth well with water and chew a piece of bland bread or cracker to cleanse your palette between each taste. This exercise can help you understand how flavors work together, and may spark your culinary creativity.

The Least You Need to Know

◆ Herbs and spices played an important role in the evolution of mankind, influencing trade, settlement, and medicine.

◆ Spices are best bought whole and ground as needed.

◆ Choose the freshest herbs you can find, and buy dried herbs often, in small quantities you can use before they go stale.

◆ Dozens of interesting flavor combinations utilize spices and herbs.

2

Spices and Herbs at Home

In This Chapter

◆ Herb gardening, indoors and out

◆ Drying and freezing herbs and spices

◆ Infusing vinegar, oil, butter, and tea

◆ Using herbs throughout your home

Once you begin investigating spices and herbs, you quickly real-
ize that they're not always easy to come by. Grocery stores stock
fresh herbs—but the herbs are frequently overpriced and often of
poor quality. Even dried herbs and spices can be weak and pale,
often having been left on the shelf for weeks or longer. As for the
more exotic spice varieties, unless you live near a major metro-
politan center, finding them is next to impossible. Sure, there are
Internet sources. But if you intend to use an herb or spice more
than once, the cost can be prohibitive.

You may have already decided that it would be well worth
your time and energy to grow your own. And luckily, most herbs

are easy crops. Grow them inside or out, from seeds or small plants, in small quantities or in huge fields. They can be preserved or used fresh. In this chapter, I show you how.

Choosing Your Crop

The hardest part about growing herbs is deciding what to plant, so why not let your recipe book dictate the herbs you choose? Several standard herbs like *thyme, mint,* and *cilantro* can be used in a multitude of cuisines. Others, like *angelica* or *costmary,* have much more limited use, but can add interest to a garden.

Consider choosing a small variety of herbs with different characteristics. Balance the stronger herbs, like *rosemary* and *basil,* with a few more delicate ones, such as *chives* and *chervil.* It's also nice to combine some hearty perennials with a few tender annuals.

Annuals are plants that bloom for one season and then die. It might seem like a waste of a good plant, but most annuals produce prolific seeds and are easily started again next season. *Biennials* live a little longer, generally two seasons, blooming in the second and then dying. *Perennials* are the long-lasting plants that, once established, bloom year after year. The tricky part of categorizing plants in this manner is that their status might change depending on your *climate zone.* While certain plants are annuals in a cooler climate, they can become biennials or even perennials where the weather is hot. Within the plant's botanical family may be several species of annuals, biennials, and perennials. In most cases, the seed or plant packaging will indicate its life span. When in doubt, ask a professional gardener.

Tidbit

Space is an important determining factor when selecting herbs to grow at home. Check the seed packet or ask the nursery staff how large your herb is likely to grow or how wide it can spread.

Knowing your climate zone is an important step in understanding what type of plants your garden can support. For the most part, your zone also indicates what plants and seeds are available to you at your local garden center. (Nurseries don't typically sell plants that won't grow.) But with today's global Internet shopping, knowing your zone can be helpful. The United States Department of Agriculture (USDA) has designated the following zones, based on the average annual minimum temperature.

Climate Zone	Temperature Range
1	below –50°F (–45.6°C)
2a	–50 to –45°F (–42.8 to –45.5°C)
2b	–45 to –40°F (–40 to –42.7°C)
3a	–40 to –35°F (–37.3 to –39.9°C)
3b	–35 to –30°F (–34.5 to –37.2°C)
4a	–30 to –25°F (–31.7 to –34.4°C)
4b	–25 to –20°F (–28.9 to –31.6°C)
5a	–20 to –15°F (–26.2 to –28.8°C)
5b	–15 to –10°F (–23.4 to –26.1°C)
6a	–10 to –5°F (–20.6 to –23.3°C)
6b	–5 to 0°F (–17.8 to –20°C)
7a	0 to 5°F (–15.0 to –17.7°C)
7b	5 to 10°F (–12.3 to –14.9°C)
8a	10 to 15°F (–9.5 to –12.2°C)
8b	15 to 20°F (–6.7 to –9.4°C)
9a	20 to 25°F (–3.9 to –6.6°C)
9b	25 to 30°F (–1.2 to –3.8°C)
10a	30 to 35°F (1.6 to –1.1°C)
10b	35 to 40°F (4.4 to 1.7°C)
11	40°F and above (4.5°C and above)

Once you identify your zone, consider your surroundings. Urban centers tend to be warmer than their surrounding areas. High elevations, where temperatures may be mild, do not promote the same growing conditions as lower elevations. High wind, high or low humidity, and the supply of sunlight should all be factored in. For more specific details about your local zone, visit a local garden center, or check out *Sunset National Garden Book* (Sunset Publishing, 1997).

Outdoor Gardens

When planning the size and shape of your garden, consider the available space, available light, and your intended crops. Choose the sunniest location you've got. For most common garden herbs, the plot should receive at least 6 hours of direct sunlight each day. More exotic species may require varying amounts of sun. Check with your local nursery staff.

Soil is the next crucial element. There's little you can do to change the amount of sun your garden receives, but poor soil can be easily amended. Your garden plot should be fertile and well drained; few herbs grow well in wet soil. Dig a hole and fill it with water. If it drains within a few minutes, your drainage is good. If it takes a few hours, you should consider planting in a raised bed.

A raised bed is essentially a giant flower pot. All you need is a frame at least 10 inches high, in any shape and made out of any material. Wood planks, logs, railroad ties, bricks, barrels, and even old tires work as sides to hold in the soil. Place your frame on the ground in your garden plot and fill it with a healthy soil mixture: $1/3$ should be composted material, whether homemade or purchased at the garden center; another $1/3$ should be sand, which lightens the mix; the remaining $1/3$ should be filled with top soil.

Tidbit

There's nothing better for your garden than compost. If you have space and patience, it's easy to make: accumulate a good mixture of green and brown yard waste, like grass clippings and dried leaves, in an unused corner of your yard or a compost bin. Add kitchen scraps like coffee grounds, egg shells, and vegetable trimmings—no meat, bones, or fat. Layer these ingredients for 3 or 4 months, watering it occasionally, and stirring it around with a pitchfork or shovel. After 4 months, the bottom and inner layers will be a nicely decomposed compost, ready to feed your garden. Remove the big chunks, and stir it into your garden soil.

If your soil drains well, it will still take a little preparation to ensure it's fertile enough to sustain your planting. Dig out your garden plot to about 1½ feet. Fill the cavity with 2 or 3 inches of crushed stone or pebbles for drainage. Create the same mixture as a raised bed, with ⅓ compost, ⅓ sand, and ⅓ topsoil, which can be the original soil from the plot or purchased. Refill the plot with your new soil mix. It will mound higher than before, which is fine and allows for settling.

Planters are a good option when space is limited. Pots, window boxes, hanging baskets, barrels, and even old buckets and wheel barrels work well. Whatever you choose, be sure it has good drainage. If your container of choice has no holes, punch some in. (For planting in containers, use the instructions that follow for indoor gardening.)

> **Hot Stuff**
>
> Don't use plastic planters in sunny locations because plastic is an insulator. It holds the heat inside the soil and can cook the plants on hot summer days.

Indoor Gardens

Planting inside is essentially the same as outside, but on a much smaller scale. The same elements are important: sunlight, drainage, and soil.

For maximum sunshine, look for a sunny window facing south or west. If light is a problem where you live, fluorescent or *grow lights* work well as a supplemental light source.

You can use any type of container as a planter, as long as it has adequate drainage holes. A layer of pebbles at the bottom of your pots keeps the soil and water from draining too quickly. Potting soil is generally rich in nutrients, so an indoor mix should consist of 1 part sand to 2 parts potting soil.

> **Chefspeak**
>
> A **grow light** produces light specifically to encourage photosynthesis. Spectrums of light can be adjusted to benefit the plant throughout its lifecycle.

Special Plantings

Why not plant a garden with a theme? You see them in arboretums all the time. Shakespeare gardens contain plants mentioned by the Bard, like Ophelia's *rosemary* from Hamlet, and *thyme* from *A Midsummer Night's Dream*. Medieval gardens are another favorite, filled with ancient medicinal herbs. Here are some practical suggestions for the culinary gardener.

Garden Theme	What to Plant
French Herb Garden	
For the bouquet garni	parsley, thyme, marjoram, leek
For fines herbes	parsley, chive, tarragon, chervil
For herbes de Provençe	chervil, marjoram, tarragon, basil, lavender, thyme
Italian Kitchen Garden	oregano, sage, rosemary, fennel, basil, garlic
Middle Eastern Garden	mint, coriander, cumin, parsley, dill, anise, oregano, thyme, sumac
Asian Garden	anise, basil, cumin, coriander, fennel, grains of paradise, ginger, cardamom, mustard, nigella (love-in-the-mist)
Barbecue Garden	celery, cumin, coriander, garlic, mustard, New Mexico chiles, oregano, onions, thyme
South-of-the-Border Garden	agave, cumin, cilantro, epazote, garlic, Mexican oregano, sage, serrano chiles

Planting

You can start herbs from seeds, or purchase small plants at a garden center or online. Small plants are the easiest way to get started, because the plant is already established and it won't take long for it to feel at home in its new pot.

For small plants, dig a hole slightly larger than the plastic pot the plant came in. Carefully remove the herb by squeezing the sides of the pot gently, turning the plant upside down, and pulling from the base of the stems. If the herb's been in the pot for a long time, it may have a lot of roots, possibly growing in and out of the pot's drainage holes. Do your best to dislodge the plant, and if necessary, cut the sides of the pot and peel it off. Loosen the roots a little by gently tearing the bottom of the pot-shaped roots open with your hands. This allows the new soil and nutrients to reach all the roots.

> **Tidbit**
>
> You can purchase a wide variety of common and not-so-common plants from these Internet suppliers: Mulberrycreek.com, Crimson-sage.com, or Mountainvalleygrowers.com.

Place the plant in the hole, pack new soil in around the top, and give it a little water. Don't drench the plant, but keep it moist and humid. Too much water makes the roots soggy and can drown the poor thing. If a good compost is used, fertilizer should not be necessary. In fact, too much fertilizer makes the foliage bushier, but reduces the herb's flavor.

Sowing Seeds

Sowing seeds is the most economical way to garden. It's easy, but it requires patience. Some seeds can be sown directly into the garden, while others benefit from indoor germination first. Check the seed packet for recommendations.

Seeds can be sown inside or out. Either way, the smaller the seed, the less soil it needs on top. Really fine seeds can be mixed with sand for more even sowing. Plan out your planting rows, and remember to leave space for you to move in. You'll need a path of some kind to access the plants once they're grown.

> **Hot Stuff**
>
> Creeping herbs, like mint, can easily take over a garden. To keep them in check, bury a large can or bucket at surface level, pierced with lots of drainage holes. Sow the seeds inside, and the can will prevent the roots from spreading willy-nilly throughout your garden.

To help germination, you can cover the seeds with burlap or newspaper to keep them moist until they sprout. If your seeds are planted outdoors, watch out after they sprout for hungry critters who like to eat tiny shoots. Fences or netting may be in order.

For indoor sowing, use a shallow planter in a sunny location. Seeds sown indoors in winter can be transplanted into the garden come spring or transferred into larger pots for indoor or outdoor gardens.

Collecting Seeds

One of the fun things about planting from seed is the endless possibilities. You are by no means limited to the plethora of packets available at your garden center. Anything with seeds in it is fair game. A weekend walk on a local trail or a visit to the farmers' market may inspire you.

Wild herbs and flowers generally produce seeds after their blooms have begun to fade. This is an indication that pollination is complete and the seeds are ripening, often inside a seed pod. Shake the withered blooms into a paper bag to loosen their seeds, or snip off the seed pod. Spread them out on trays to dry completely.

Tidbit

Tomato seeds need special treatment. They must be soaked in water for 3 or 4 days to ferment. After that time, the good ones will have sunk to the bottom of the dish. Dry them out completely before storing or planting.

You can also find seeds inside fleshy fruits and vegetables. Remove, rinse, and spread the seeds on trays a single layer to dry.

Once dried, plant your seeds or store them, well labeled, in paper envelopes. Exotic, wild, and heirloom seeds such as these make for an interesting garden, as well as a fun gift for your gardening friends.

Extended Care

As your herbs grow, you'll want to utilize them for your culinary creations. For the best flavor, harvest the leaves just before the flower buds open. If the plant is outdoors, harvest in the morning, before the dew has evaporated. These conditions produce the most aromatic oils within the plants leaves.

If you have no use for the herbs right now, prune them as if you did (and then freeze or dry the herb; more on this coming up in later sections). A regular trim keeps your plants producing healthy, flavorful foliage.

Annuals die off after the first season, but perennials and biennials last longer, which means you must consider winter care. Unless the temperature in your area dips below 0 for prolonged periods, most herbs survive well with mulching. Cover the ground around the plant with straw, leaves, or pine needles. (Branches from your Christmas tree work great.) Mulching isn't necessary for plants that die back, like *chives*, *mint*, and *tarragon*. They prefer a month or two of freezing temperature to regenerate next year's growth.

In colder climates, you can dig up and pot your herbs for a winter indoors. Prune branches and trim the inner foliage to let light and air circulate. Rinse off any bugs, and plant the herbs in roomy pots, using 1 part sand to 2 parts potting soil. Keep the herbs in a sunny location and prune regularly. Replant them in the garden when spring warms up your dirt.

Potted perennials and biennials, whether indoor or outdoor, grow as time goes by. Make them comfy by moving them into larger containers from time to time.

Tidbit

It is entirely possible that you have neither ample garden space outside, nor optimal conditions inside. Never fear! There are more than 15,000 community gardens throughout the United States and Canada. To find one in your area, check your local city administration or visit the American Community Garden Association at communitygarden.org.

Preserving Flavor

Using herbs in your kitchen is great, but when supply exceeds demand, it seems a shame to let all that flavor go to waste. That's where herb preservation comes in.

In the olden days, people were forced to eat bland foods in the winter if they failed to preserve summer's bounty. But today, just because the basil is at its peak doesn't necessarily mean you have time to use it *right now*. If you have a little spare time, you can set the flavor aside for later.

Drying Herbs

Moisture removal is essential for preservation of herbs. For best results, harvest your herbs right before they flower, when they're at the peak of flavor. Cut them in the morning before the dew has dried, when their oils are at their highest concentration. Trim the stems of perennials about halfway down the stem, and cut annuals at ground level. Wash the stems and leaves thoroughly in cool running water to remove dirt and bugs. Shake them off and spread them out in a single layer on paper towels to dry completely for a couple hours. When the rinse water has evaporated, the real drying can begin.

You can dry herbs naturally or with the help of a microwave, dehydrator, or oven. If time and space allow, natural drying is preferred, as the herbs retain more of the natural oils.

Natural Drying

Hanging herbs is a great drying method if you have the space. Gravity helps the oils flow from the stem into the leaves, giving your dried herbs maximum flavor.

Tie small bunches of herbs together tightly at the stems with a rubber band or wire twist-tie, and hang them in a clean, well-ventilated spot. The herbs will be ready to store in about 2 weeks, when the leaves are brittle.

To preserve more of the herb's natural color, place them in a paper bag, with the stems exposed, before tying and hanging. To collect the herbs when they're dried, simply shake the bag and remove the stems.

Tray drying works, too, although it is a little more labor-intensive. Remove the leaves from the stems and spread them out in a

> **Hot Stuff**
>
> Be sure the room where you hang your herbs to dry is no warmer than 80 degrees or you'll find yourself with moldy herbs.

single layer on trays or screens. Store them in a dark, ventilated room, and turn the leaves over every few days to dry evenly.

Salt curing is another method of naturally preserving herbs. Layer clean and dried leaves with regular table salt or kosher salt in a shallow pan or dish. Be sure the leaves are completely covered. In 2 or 3 weeks, remove the leaves, shake off the salt, and test the leaves for a brittle texture.

Ovens and Dehydrators

Speed is the only advantage to using ovens to dry herbs. And it's tricky because the herbs are actually being cooked. But if monitored carefully, the results are pretty good.

To dry in the microwave, layer rinsed and dried herbs between two paper towels. Cook on a medium setting for about 3 minutes, checking frequently until the herbs are dry and brittle. Stir them a bit if they seem to be drying unevenly.

Herbs can also be dried in a regular oven at very low temperatures. Layer them on baking sheets and bake at 150°F for 2 or 3 hours, stirring periodically for even drying. To test for doneness, remove a leaf from the oven. It will be crisper when it cools.

Hot Stuff

It's easy to overcook and brown the herbs when drying them in the oven, so watch them carefully.

Dehydrators are another option. They don't heat up as much as an oven, they don't actually cook the herbs like a microwave does, and they don't require constant monitoring. To use, spread the leaves out in the trays in a single layer and follow the manufacturer's instructions. Generally, herbs will completely dry in a dehydrator after a few hours.

Storing Dried Herbs

The purpose of drying herbs is to remove the moisture so they can be stored for long periods of time without deteriorating. After putting in all the effort to grow and dry your herbs, be sure to store them properly in airtight containers. I prefer canning jars with lids that seal tightly. Don't use paper or cardboard, as they will absorb the herbs' oil. Seeds and leaves should be left whole to retain as much flavor as possible. They will last for months stored this way and kept in a cool, dark cupboard.

Hot Stuff

Even if the herbs appear dry, it's always possible that they could have retained a little moisture. Check the jars every day for the first week or so for any sign of moisture. If you see condensation or signs of any mold, remove the herbs and repeat the drying process.

Freezing Herbs

One way to preserve the fresh-picked flavor of your herbs is to freeze them. Once frozen, herbs are not pretty enough for garnish, but they work well in most recipes.

To freeze herbs, first wash and dry them and strip the leaves off the stems. Chop the leaves fine, as you would for a recipe. Divide the herbs into small quantities, as you would likely use in one recipe, such as 1 or 2 tablespoons. Put them into small plastic zipper bags, and force out the air before you seal it to minimize the formation of ice crystals. Label each bag so you can identify the herb later.

You could also place 1 or 2 tablespoons of the chopped herb into each section of an ice cube tray, cover with water, and freeze. After the cubes are frozen, remove them from the tray and store in labeled zipper bags.

Tidbit

Freezing herbs in ice cube trays only works for recipes that can stand a little extra water, like soups or stews. It won't work for preparations like chicken salad that would get soggy with the extra moisture.

Herbs can also be frozen in a purée form, as with pesto. Using a blender, purée herbs with just enough oil to get the mixture moving. Freeze in small plastic tubs or ice cube trays.

Blending Tea

Tea is an excellent use of dried spices and herbs. Besides the everyday chamomile or mint, why not try an original concoction? I like to use ¼ cup spices and herbs for every 3 cups not quite boiling water. The following table lists some of my favorite blends. (Measurements are given in parts so they can be made easily in any quantity. All ingredients are dried, unless otherwise specified.)

Tea Blend	Ingredients
Floral Tea	1 part each rose petals, violets, lavender buds, orange blossoms, red bergamot
Tummy-Soothing After-Dinner Teaseed	2 parts peppermint; 1 part each fennel seed, anise seed, lemon balm
Exotic Spiced Tea	2 parts rose petals; 1 part each fennel, cardamom, peppermint; 1 cinnamon stick; 1 slice fresh ginger
Refreshing Spa Tea	1 part each rosemary, sage, mint, lemon myrtle (Serve over ice and sliced cucumber.)
Citrus Tea	3 parts kaffir lime leaves; 2 parts lemon grass or lemon verbena; 1 part each orange blossom, allspice; 1 cinnamon stick (Serve with a wedge of orange.)

To brew the tea, crush and chop the spices and herbs just before the hot water is added, and let it steep for 5 minutes. Strain into your cup, use a tea ball, or make your own tea bags from cheesecloth. Don't forget—the tea can be served hot or cold!

A Garden in Your Pantry

An easy way to preserve the flavor of herbs is to infuse them into oil or vinegar. Oils and fats carry flavor in recipes, so any flavor infused into oil spreads throughout the dish, often more than the herb would on its own. And because vinegars are acidic, they accentuate the flavors they're infused with.

Flavored vinegars and oils make terrific salad dressings. But don't just limit their use to salad greens. Roasted root vegetables, slow cooked beans, and even fruits benefit from these bright flavors. By themselves they make delicious marinades or great dips for veggies and breads, and they add something extra to your everyday cooking.

Safety First

Infused oils and vinegars make wonderful gifts. But you don't want to give your friends *E. coli* or *botulism*. As with any type of food canning, sanitation is critical. Everything the oils and vinegars come in contact with needs to be impeccably clean. This begins with the herbs themselves. Fresh herbs, especially those you didn't grow yourself, should be thoroughly cleaned. To be sure no bacteria are present, a quick dip in a sanitizing solution is recommended. The FDA recommends 1 teaspoon household bleach dissolved in 6 cups water. (Diluting and rinsing make this perfectly safe.) Dip the herbs in and then rinse them in cold running water. Dry them completely before adding to oils.

While there are many attractive decorative bottles available, it's easier to make your infusions in wide-mouth canning jars first and then strain them into the pretty bottles. Jars, bottles, lids, and corks must all be sanitized before you begin. The easiest way to do this is to run them through a dishwasher. Another easy method is to set the jars and lids in boiling water and cook them for 10 minutes. Carefully remove them from the boil with tongs and allow them to drain and cool on clean towels before filling.

Flavored oils and vinegars are often seen gracing the counters of well-groomed kitchens and gourmet shops. But it takes more than a decorative sprig to get the flavorful infusions that make a difference in your recipes. For both oils and vinegar, herbs should be chopped, bruised, and packed tightly into glass jars, filling them at least $^3/_4$ full. The more leaves you use, and the more they are bruised, the more aromatic oil escapes into the infusion.

Flavored Vinegars

Infused vinegars show off the herbs and spices best if the vinegar chosen is light in flavor. Distilled white vinegar is too harsh, but white wine vinegar is a good choice, as is rice vinegar. Cider vinegar can work, too, if the spices and herbs are strong in flavor. Red wine and balsamic vinegar are much too strong, and their flavor will compete with your infusions.

Thoroughly cleaning and sanitizing the herbs and jars is an important step in preventing E. coli contamination. To ensure no harmful bacteria are present, bring your vinegar to a simmer before pouring it into a sanitized jar packed with herbs and spices. Cover it loosely with cheesecloth or a clean towel. When completely cool, seal it with a sterilized lid and set it in a cool dark spot for 2 to 4 weeks to infuse.

When you think its ready, strain out the herbs and give the vinegar a taste. If it's not strong enough, repeat the process with a new batch of chopped herbs. If it tastes ready, strain out any small particles and cloudiness through a coffee filter or several layers of cheesecloth. Place a few decorative sprigs of clean herbs inside a sanitized decorative bottle and fill with the vinegar. Seal with a sanitized cork or cap.

> **Hot Stuff**
>
> Be sure the bottle seal is not made of metal or rubber, which are both easily corroded by acid.

You can use a single herb or spice to create a terrific flavored vinegar, but don't overlook the combinations in the following table. They can stand alone as a dressing, glaze, or dip. (Measurements are given in parts so they can be made easily in any quantity. All herbs are used fresh, unless otherwise specified.)

Flavored Vinegar	Ingredients
Garden Herb Vinegar	4 parts parsley; 3 parts chives; 2 parts each thyme, tarragon; 1 part each sage, celery seed; white wine vinegar

continues

continued

Flavored Vinegar	Ingredients
Chile Spice Vinegar	3 parts dried guajillo chiles; 2 parts each coriander, cumin; 1 part each garlic, thyme, oregano, cumin; cider vinegar
Minted Vinegar	2 parts each peppermint, spearmint, wintergreen; 1 part each lemon verbena, anise seed; 1 part sugar; rice vinegar
Winter Spice Vinegar	2 parts each rosemary, thyme; 1 part each mint, allspice berries, chopped ginger, cardamom; 1 cinnamon stick; 3 cloves; 1 tonka bean or $1/4$ vanilla bean; white wine vinegar
Eastern Vinegar	3 parts each kaffir lime leaves, cilantro, scallion; 2 parts toasted sesame seed; 1 part each chopped garlic, chopped ginger, star anise, Szechwan peppercorns; rice vinegar
Fruit Vinegar	3 parts raspberries; 1 part each opal basil, lemon verbena, lemon thyme; 1 cinnamon stick; white wine vinegar

Flavored Oils

The preparation for infusing spices and herbs into oil is similar to that of vinegar, but the dangers are a little different. Acidic vinegar is an inhospitable environment for botulism, but a little moisture trapped in an oxygen-free bottle of oil is a perfect host. Sanitizing the bottles and herbs is an important step, but further precaution should be taken, too. Take care to completely dry foods you plan to infuse into the oil. Oil with infusions of foods like garlic or chiles, with a lot of internal moisture, are especially susceptible to botulism. Make these oils in small batches and store them in the refrigerator. If they haven't been used in 2 weeks, freeze or discard them.

To accentuate the flavors of the spices and herbs in your oil, choose a neutral oil as your base, one that has a very light, nondescript flavor, such as canola, safflower, or vegetable oil. Unlike infused vinegars, oil should not be heated before it's infused. Pour it cool into a sanitized jar of clean spices and chopped herbs. Seal it tightly with a sanitized lid and let it sit in a cool dark spot for 2 weeks. Shake the jar daily to blend the aromatic oils with the base oil. After 2 weeks, taste the oil. If the flavor is lacking, strain the oil into another sterilized jar full of spices and herbs and repeat the process.

> **Tidbit**
> Olive oil and nut oils are generally too strong for flavored oils ... unless you want the flavor of the olives and the nuts to be a part of your flavor blend.

The following table lists some ideas for uniquely flavored oils. Drizzle them over grilled meat and seafood, roasted vegetables, or cook with them instead of your plain old olive oil. They are guaranteed to spice up your meal. (Measurements are given in parts so they can be made easily in any quantity. All herbs are used fresh, unless otherwise specified.)

Flavored Oil	Ingredients
Herbaceous Olive Oil	2 parts each rosemary, basil, sage; 1 part each chopped garlic, fennel seed, basil; 1 pequin chile; olive oil
Spicy Barbecue Oil	2 parts each oregano, thyme, cilantro; 1 part each cumin, coriander, chile arbol, kaffir lime leaves, brown sugar, garlic, mustard seed; 1 cinnamon stick; peanut oil
Savory Oil for Seafood	2 parts each bay leaves, celery seeds; 1 part each cardamom, allspice, chopped ginger; 1 vanilla bean; 1 cinnamon stick; corn oil
Lemon Pepper Oil	3 parts lemongrass; 1 part each pink peppercorn, Szechwan peppercorn, chopped ginger; corn oil

continues

continued

Flavored Oil	Ingredients
Annatto Oil	1 part each annatto seed, garlic, sautéed in an equal amount of safflower oil until warmed and then cooled completely; 1 part each bay leaves, cinnamon sticks, black pepper; safflower oil
Caribbean Oil	2 parts each juniper berries, cilantro, thyme; 1 part each chopped garlic, chopped ginger; 1 scotch bonnet chile; 1 cinnamon stick; peanut oil

Compound Butter

Adding spices and herbs to butter is an unexpected way to incorporate their aromatic essence into a recipe. Flavored butters can be used as a sauce melted over broiled fish, grilled meats, steamed vegetables, potatoes, or noodles. They can also become part of another recipe. Add them into a sauce, use them in baking, or simply set them on the table as an accompaniment to your dinner rolls.

For best results, start with room temperature unsalted butter. For every pound of butter, you can add up to 1½ cups of flavorings. Mince the herbs very fine, and grind the spices. Stir the flavorings into the softened butter thoroughly. Be sure anything that has been heated, such as sautéed shallots, is completely cooled before it's added to the butter. Roll the butter into a 1- or 2-inch thick log on a piece of parchment paper or waxed paper. Wrap the paper around the butter log and twist the ends tightly, like a sausage. Chill your compound butter completely or freeze for up to a week.

Hot Stuff

Don't add more than the recommended quantity of spices and herbs, or the butter will lose its structural integrity and fall apart too easily when it's cut or spread.

To use your butter, unwrap and slice off $1/2$-inch coins. For an alternate presentation, pipe the butter through a pastry bag fitted with a decorative tip into rosettes. As an accompaniment to baked goods, pack it into small ramekins and chill, or roll it into butter balls and serve it in a small dish over a few ice cubes.

The classic compound butter is Beurre Maître d'Hôtel (see recipe in Chapter 4 under *Parsley*), but you need not be limited to that old standard. Try some of the ideas in the following table or create your own. (Measurements are given in parts so they can be made easily in any quantity. All herbs are used fresh, unless otherwise specified. Use unsalted butter, but add a pinch of salt for every pound of butter to bring out the natural flavors.)

Compound Butter	Ingredients
Flower Butter	1 part each rose petals, lavender buds, violets
Gingerbread Butter	2 parts each ground cinnamon, ground nutmeg; 1 part each ground cardamom, ground nutmeg, ground allspice; grated zest of 1 orange and 1 lemon
Pesto Butter	3 parts basil; 1 part each parsley, chervil, chopped garlic, toasted walnuts
Roasted Pepper Butter	3 parts cilantro; 2 parts each epazote, cumin, ground white peppercorns, chopped garlic; 1 Anaheim chile, roasted, peeled and chopped fine
Lemon Mint Butter	1 part each peppermint, lemon balm, lemon thyme, ground pink peppercorns; zest of 1 lemon

Fragrance Throughout Your Home

Spices and herbs were used to heal and cleanse long before we began adding them to our food. The recent boom in aromatherapy is nothing new at all. Here are some easy, nonedible ways to utilize your bountiful harvest.

Potpourri

Placed about a room in decorative bowls, or sewn tight into sachet pillows, the colorful dried petals of *potpourri* are a wonderfully aromatic use for your spices and herbs.

Chefspeak

The word *potpourri* means "rotten pot," and that's what it was. Ceramic and porcelain lidded containers were filled with herbs, spices, and some distilled spirits. The vegetation would emit fragrance as it decomposed. The containers were set near the fire, and the lid was lifted when someone entered the room. Small potpourri buckets were even hung about one's person, tucked under petticoats for fragrance to go.

Dry the herbs as described earlier in this chapter. Flowers and flower petals can be dried in a similar manner. Thick flower heads, like roses, are best broken apart and dried as individual petals. Whole roses and rose buds can be used, but take care that they have dried completely. It's essential to thoroughly dry all your potpourri ingredients. The tiniest amount of moisture left in a leaf, if buried in the mix, can easily turn to mold and spread very quickly.

Tidbit

Many recipes for potpourri include a small amount of imitation fragrance. As with imitation flavorings, the effect is good, but not necessarily natural. A well-chosen mixture of freshly dried natural ingredients can lend just as much fragrance as any imitation oil. Be sure to stir the mixture occasionally to break up the ingredients and release the natural oils.

Sachets, Simmers, and Soaks

A small amount is all that's needed to add fragrance to a room. Fill a bowl with a cup or two, and keep the unused potpourri stored in an airtight container. An even smaller amount can be sewn into small fabric pillows to make fragrant sachets. Tuck them into dresser drawers, linen cupboards, and suitcases. Hang them in closets, bathrooms, laundry rooms, and from your rearview mirror. Or simmer potpourri on the stove. This method is a good idea in dry climates, where the aromatic oils tend to dissipate quickly into the air.

Herbal mixtures can be used to fragrance yourself, too. Combine soothing blends in a muslin bag and toss it in the tub for a soothing bath, or add to your hand-washing rinse water. Mix them with Epsom salts for a skin-softening foot soak, or combine them with vinegar for a refreshing skin toner.

Freshen each room in your home with the essence of your garden. Seasonal availability can also dictate your ingredients. Use the recipes in the following table as a guide and then come up with your own blends. (Measurements are given in parts so they can be made easily in any quantity. All herbs are used dried.)

Potpourri Blend	Ingredients
Floral Potpourri	4 parts rose petals; 2 parts lavender buds; 1 part each rosemary, lemon verbena, tarragon, allspice
Citrus Spice Potpourri	3 parts each dried orange peel, myrtle blossoms; 2 parts each bay leaf, rosemary, peppermint; 1 part each cinnamon stick, fennel seed, cloves; 1 tonka bean or $1/4$ vanilla bean
Autumn Potpourri	2 parts each pine needles, rosemary, bay leaves; 1 part each cinnamon stick, clove, allspice, orange peel, rose petals (Use this as a steaming potpourri as well.)
Headache Sachet	3 parts lavender; 2 parts rosemary; 1 part each lemon thyme, lemon verbena, sage, woodruff
Refreshing Face Wash	1 part each chamomile, rose petals, lavender, lemon balm, thyme, white vinegar (Steep in 6 parts warm water for 15 minutes before use.)
Soothing Herbal Bath	2 parts Epsom salt; 1 part each rosemary, lavender, peppermint, lemon verbena (Mix and store in an airtight container for 1 week before use.)

Your recipes take on a whole new dimension when you consider the meanings of your ingredients:

Basil = good wishes

Bay = victory

Borage = courage

Caraway = remembrance

Chamomile = comfort

Cloves = dignity

Coriander = hidden worth

Cumin = engagement

Hyssop = cleanliness

Dill = power against witchcraft

Fennel = strength

Juniper = protection

Lavender = luck

Lemon verbena = unity

Marjoram = happiness

Mugwort = happy travels

Myrtle = true love

Oregano = joy

Parsley = festive

Peppermint = affection

Rose = love

Rosemary = remembrance

Rue = protection

Sage = wisdom

Thyme = courage

Violet = faithfulness

Wormwood = absence

Yarrow = everlasting love

Once you discover all the pleasure spices and herbs can add to your everyday life, be sure to share them with friends. Gifts made from herbs and spices are especially cherished when they're made with love. You can even choose herbs with special meanings to personalize your gifts.

The Least You Need to Know

◆ For the best and freshest selection of spices and herbs, grow them yourself.

◆ Herbs are easy to cultivate outdoors or in.

◆ Preserve the essence of home-grown spices and herbs with careful drying, freezing, infusion into vinegar and oils, and blending into butter and tea.

◆ Dried spices and herbs can be used throughout your home to add freshness and fragrance in unexpected places.

Chapter 3

The Science of Flavor

In This Chapter

- ◆ Mapping the tongue
- ◆ The basic elements of taste
- ◆ Combining senses to determine flavor

Someone with a sense of style is said to "have good taste." Calling something "tasteful" is a compliment. As modern humans, we have evolved away from the survival values of basic taste to a notion that taste is primarily a sense of pleasure. Eating is no longer simply about the need to sustain life. It is a cultural, social, and familial event, built around flavor.

Let's explore taste and flavor. They are different, but intertwined.

Stick Out Your Tongue

At the turn of the twentieth century, German research scientist D. P. Hänig published a map of the tongue. It illustrated the tongue perimeter and the intensity of sensitivity to four basic sensations: sweet, salty, bitter, and sour. The original drawings show clearly that the entire perimeter of the tongue was sensitive to all flavors but that certain areas had greater sensitivity to one of the four specific sensations.

The Tongue Map

From that first map evolved the simple tongue map seen in textbooks across the country. No longer were the tastes perceived around the entire tongue. Instead, the sensation of bitter was focused in the back of the tongue, sweet on the tip, salt on the front sides, and sour on the back sides.

If you've ever tried to experiment with taste based on this map, you'll know right away that it's false. You taste things throughout your *entire* mouth. The modern tongue map is now widely refuted.

Tidbit

Debunk the tongue map yourself. Gather a few elements representing each basic taste, like salt, lemon juice, cold coffee, and sugar. Taste them, one at a time. Swirl the taste throughout your entire mouth, and concentrate on where you feel the taste. Rinse your mouth well with water and chew a piece of bland bread or cracker to cleanse your palette between each taste. Carefully record your findings.

How Your Taste Buds Work

Your tongue, soft palate, and epiglottis are covered with about 10,000 taste buds. They are found on those visible bumps, called *papillae*. Each taste bud has about 100 taste cells, on which are taste receptors. The things we taste include a number of molecular structures, such as ions, organic molecules, carbohydrates, amino acids, and proteins. The molecules are carried by saliva into the receptors, which respond to a few basic taste sensations and transmit the taste information to the brain.

Each taste bud recognizes all the taste sensations. Each one has a preference and responds to one of the tastes more strongly than the others. But the increased sensitivity is minor and not nearly as defined as the modern tongue map would have us believe.

Humans inherit different levels of sensory responsiveness, which influences what we eat. Some taste less, some more. Babies and the elderly have less tolerance for strong tastes. Hormones affect how we taste and what we crave. (Consider the eating habits of pregnant women and teenagers.) Drugs, both legal and illegal, affect our sense of taste and alter our perception of flavor.

 Tidbit

Some people called super-tasters perceive taste with intense reaction. For them, capsaicin, bitterness, and artificial sweeteners are not easily tolerated.

An Explanation of Taste

We eat the foods we like, and avoid the ones we don't. But why? And why do some people love foods that others despise? Our preferences stem from physiological traits that have evolved with our species. It started as a means for survival. Taste drives our appetite. We crave certain foods because our body needs them. Sweets are rich in energy-giving carbohydrates. Salt balances our body fluids and carries nutrition throughout the body. Bitterness and acidity are warnings of toxins and spoiled foods. Nature is an amazing thing.

Of course, our cave-dwelling ancestors didn't crave a Milky Way bar like you do, and most would have quickly spat out that cup of coffee because taste has evolved in humans over time as a result of technological and cultural events. For instance, the ability to preserve foods through curing (salt) and brining (acid) changed our reluctance to ingest these basic tastes. We taught ourselves to like alcohol and coffee (fermented, bitter, and astringent beverages) because we found their effects pleasurable. People brought up with a diet of highly spiced foods have a much higher tolerance for it. Much of the body's natural defense mechanisms have been thwarted in the name of flavor.

In deconstructing flavor, we divide foods into four taste groups based on the sensory capabilities of our tongue: salty, sour, sweet, and bitter. But the basic elements of flavor are classified differently from culture to culture. *Hot* is an added taste sensation in China. India adds *spicy* and *astringent*. The Japanese term *umami*, meaning "delicious flavor" and also called *savory* or *succulent*, has recently been accepted around the world as a legitimate taste element. At the University of Burgundy, researchers have isolated a taste receptor for *fat*. Some consider *metallic* a taste, especially after experiencing their tongue on the flag pole or accidentally chewing aluminum foil. There even those who identify *neutral* as a taste, as in water. The number of primary tastes is up for some debate, so let's start by identifying the obvious ones.

> **Tidbit**
>
> Inability to taste is called *ageusia*. Older people often suffer from a reduced ability to taste, called *hypoagusia*, caused by slow rejuvenation of taste receptor cells. Increased use of medications can also cause this condition.

Salty

Saltiness is mainly experienced in the presence of sodium chloride (NaCl). Sodium is necessary for physiological survival to keep the concentration of our body fluids at the correct levels. It helps our cells absorb nutrients, and it helps transmit electrical impulses to our nerves. Like sugar, it's possible that the craving for salt is a built-in survival reflex.

Sodium naturally occurs in meats, so people and animals who eat mostly plants can easily become deficient. Overconsumption of sodium is problematic, too, causing dehydration and retention of water that can lead to high blood pressure.

Salt is universally used to bring out the natural flavors of foods. When used correctly, the food should taste deliciously like itself and not a salty version of itself. One reason for this effect from salt could be the way the sensation is transmitted. The receptor for salt is an ion channel that allows sodium ions to pass directly through the cell membrane, creating the sensory perception of saltiness. Acid, another taste used to brighten the flavor of foods, penetrates the cells in the same way. Sweet and bitter substances, however, must wind through the cell membrane several times before they're perceived. This direct perception may explain the ability of salt and acid to wake up our taste buds and brighten food's flavor.

The effect that salt has on the balance of flavors is vital in the kitchen. If you've ever had a meal devoid of salt, you'll know what I mean. Bread, pasta, and meats prepared without salt are bland and nondescript. Salt vastly improves all recipes, enhancing the natural flavor of everything from lettuce to chocolate cake.

Hot Stuff

Salt absorbs moisture from the air just as it absorbs moisture from food. This can be problematic for your salt shaker if you live in a humid environment. To combat clumpy salt in your shaker, add a few grains of rice. The rice will absorb the moisture and keep the salt dry.

Salt also reduces the bitterness of foods by actually changing your perception of it. You can test this by adding a little salt to bitter tonic water. Just before it begins to taste salty, the quinine tastes sweet.

Chemically, salt plays a role in several key culinary applications. If added to water, it will raise the temperature of the boil and lower the temperature of the freeze. The use of rock salt in old-fashioned ice-cream machines is an example of this chilling effect.

In bread making, salt inhibits the growth of yeast. Without a carefully controlled amount of salt, the yeast would feed uncontrollably and produce an unpleasant, overly fermented flavor.

Salt has been used as a preservative for centuries because it draws out moisture. The process is called *salt-curing*. Fish and meat packed in salt release moisture, creating an unsuitable environment for bacterial growth. It was an early method for transporting foods on long journeys. This dehydration is the principle behind koshered meats. During the butchering process, the meat is heavily salted, releasing all body fluids. For this reason, too, meat stays juicier if it's left unsalted until cooking is complete. Salt draws the moisture out of vegetables and fruits in the same way.

Sour

Sour taste seems to be innately unpleasant. This is by design, as soured foods, like spoiled milk and rotten fruit, tend to make us ill. But as children age, there tends to be a period in which the sour taste is highly prized (which explains the popularity of sour gummy worms).

In cooking, acid is used to wake up flavor, much like salt is. It makes us salivate, which is a necessary step in moving taste to the receptors and in digestion. In our stomach, acid encourages production of hydrochloric acid for digestion. (This is why vinaigrette salads are served at the beginning of a meal.) Acid has an antifungal effect and is often referred to as the disinfectant of the intestines.

The particular health benefits of vinegar include lowering blood pressure and suppressing lactic acid build-up. In Japan, vinegar cafés are popping up in train stations, serving beverages made with vinegar, fruits, and vegetables to health-conscious commuters.

Tidbit

Try this experiment with salt and acid: take a bland food, like an avocado, and divide it into three portions. Sprinkle one portion with a pinch of salt, one with a drop of lemon juice, and leave the third one alone. Taste the difference in flavor the salt and acid makes, and compare it to the plain avocado.

Every cuisine utilizes the acidic pucker. Vinegar, lemon, lime, *tamarind*, *amchoor*, gooseberries, *tomatillos*, and *sorrel* all lend a sour edge to food and make it characteristic of the country in question. Tart beverages are common all over the world, too, like *aguas frescas* in Mexico, made with sugar and tamarind, or *citron presse* in France, which is nothing more than a glass of straight lemon juice with a side of water and sugar. The pucker is so desirable that chefs incorporate citric acid as an ingredient to up the pucker factor of their recipes.

Tidbit

Carnivores, like cats, are unable to recognize sweetness. In the wild, they're strictly meat eaters, so they have evolved without the sweet taste receptor. Dogs choose sugar water over plain, but not cats. Test it on your own pets.

Sweet

Human babies respond to sugar quite early. The taste is innately pleasant because the calorie-rich carbohydrates are an essential energy source for humans.

Sweetness works with other tastes in interesting ways. Acidic and bitter foods are made palatable by sugars. If you need proof, think about coffee or lemon pie. Chocolate is another great example. No one likes to eat unsweetened chocolate, but just a little sugar creates bitter-sweet and semisweet, craved by chocoholics worldwide.

But excess sweetness drastically changes the sensation of the other tastes. This is why sweet wines and desserts are best enjoyed at the end of a meal.

Conversely, sweetness is tamed by acid and bitterness. Chefs commonly use acid to cut the cloying sweetness of certain recipes, including candies, fruits, and sweet vegetables like yams.

> **Tidbit**
>
> *Miraculin* is a protein found in the small red berries of the West African *miracle fruit plant*. It has no flavor of its own, but it makes sour foods taste sweet for up to an hour. The miracle fruit has long been used to improve the flavor of sour food.

We think of sweet as being derived from sugar (sucrose), but other naturally sweet compounds are even sweeter, such as *licorice root* and *angelica*.

Bitter

Bitterness is meant to be a warning against toxicity. Sharp, disagreeable tastes occur as a natural indication of poison. Synthetic, bitter-tasting chemicals are commonly added to toxic substances like antifreeze and denatured alcohol to prevent accidental poisoning. Nail-biting remedies employ a similar tactic. But as humans evolved, we learned to ignore the bitter warnings. The so-called *acquired* or *grown-up* flavors of coffee and alcohol are essentially toxic, especially in large quantities. But because we enjoy the effects, we add sugar, acid, and other flavorings to make them palatable.

Herbivores have an altered sensitivity to bitterness as a means of survival. Their bodies have adapted to allow the ingestion of toxins that would cause adverse reaction in the rest of us. This provides them with a much wider variety of food options.

Umami

Scientists have recently isolated taste receptors that respond to glutemic acids, or glutamates. First found in seaweed, glutamates are used in the flavor enhancer *monosodium glutamate* (*MSG*). Some call it the fifth taste, while others still refer to it as more of a mouthfeel. It's taste has been described in several ways, including meaty, savory, succulent, woodsy, and earthy.

Glutamates drive our appetite for amino acids, the building block of protein, which is essential for tissue repair. It's found in meats, as well as fermented and aged foods like cheese, fish sauce, and mushrooms.

Sensing Flavor

Knowing that there are only a few basic tastes, you may have concluded by now that there's more to flavor than just your tongue.

The Nose Knows

Although the tongue can distinguish a handful of tastes, the nose can differentiate hundreds of substances in minute quantities. If you doubt the importance your sense of smell plays in flavor, think back to the last time you had a bad cold. The texture of the chicken soup was warm and soothing, but could you really taste it? For this reason, good chefs never wear cologne.

Tidbit

Test the power of your nose. Peel and dice a potato and an apple. Mix them up, plug your nose, close your eyes, and pick a piece to eat. Can you tell which it is?

There are more than 1,000 olfactory receptors in the upper part of the nasal cavity. They can distinguish the nuances of essential oils, esters, and other aromatic compounds that make up the world around us. If you really want to taste something, chew it, close your mouth, and exhale through your nose. This forces the aromatic compounds through the pharynx, past the largest concentration of olfactory receptors, giving you the most flavor possible.

Mouthfeel

Much of how food is described is based on feel in addition to flavor. During chewing, you perceive pressure throughout your mouth. Your *somatosensory system* detects multiple sensations from the body, including touch and pressure, temperature, pain, itch, and tickle. From the mouth, this system sends impulses to the brain, which, in cases of shockingly sweet, tart, or bitter foods, may result in jaw pain, tongue thrusting, puckering, and shuddering. Crunchy, crispy, chewy, soggy, juicy, and slimy all conjure up very specific food traits. Whether these sensations are good or bad is entirely determined by your expectations. Juicy may be pleasant in an apple, but not necessarily in a cookie.

> **Hot Stuff**
>
> Take care when describing your culinary creations. Use *moist* instead of *wet, crisp* instead of *hard,* and *mild* instead of *bland.*

The touch and pressure of food in the mouth is typically referred to as *mouthfeel.* The Japanese call it *Kokumi,* or "thickness." Chefs strive to create dishes with pleasant mouthfeel by combining textures in an agreeable way, such as crispy cookies with creamy custards. Of course, what's pleasurable to one is not necessarily pleasurable to all. Take carbonated beverages, for example. Many find effervescence very unpleasant, even painful. Gelatin is another food with a texture folks either love or hate.

> **Tidbit**
>
> As a culinary instructor, I was constantly testing my students' palettes. My favorite examination was the blind taste test. I carefully gathered an assortment of spices and herbs and ground or chopped them to similar consistency. Each was numbered and placed in a small paper cup. Students tasted each one and tried to identify them. Try it yourself and test your *taste IQ.*

Astringency is a dryness brought about by foods that contain tannins. Derived from seeds, skins, bark, leaves, and unripened fruits, tannins constrict the tissue of any part of the mouth they come in contact with. Examples of tannic, astringent foods include aged red wines, hops, and tea. Unripened persimmons are especially known for their astringency.

The effects of astringency sound unpleasant, but consider what tannins can do when combined with other foods. Hoppy beer with fried foods, red wines with fatty meats, and tea with scones and clotted cream are all classic combinations that use astringency to cut through fats and expose more of the food's flavor.

Temperature

One of the easiest ways to alter the flavor of food is with temperature. A temperature change can alter flavor, texture, and even render some food unpalatable. Coldness tends to subdue all flavors. Cheese, beer, meats, vegetables, and fruits are always better if allowed to warm up a bit after they've come out of the fridge. As the temperature increases, more odor molecules are released and can be detected. (This is not only true for food. Consider dumpsters—and people.)

Tidbit

Test the effect temperature has on food by scooping out a dish of ice cream and letting it melt at room temperature. Then taste it side by side with frozen ice cream. The low temperature subdues the sweetness. You can test this with warm and cold soda pop, too.

Some sugar substitutes have been shown to actually change temperature on the tongue, but most temperature changes are false. Certain foods trick the tongue into thinking there has been a temperature change by activating the same nerve cells that actual temperature changes activate.

False heat, also referred to as *spicy* or *piquant*, is best exemplified by capsaicin, the compound found in chile peppers. Similar reactions occur with black pepper, cinnamon (as in red-hot candies), mustard oil (wasabi and hot mustard), eugenol (clove oil), and ethanol (distilled alcohol). *False cooling* is found in menthol, spearmint, and camphor (think vapor rub). These effects can be put to great use in the kitchen, as in cooling mint beverages and warming spiced ciders.

Eat With Your Eyes

Let us not neglect the importance of vision in our enjoyment of foods. Few things in the world are more exciting than having a beautiful plate of food set in front of you. But besides the obvious appreciation of an artistically designed presentation, what we see has a lot to do with what we taste. Our brain has specific expectations regarding color and food, and when those expectations are not met, our body reacts physically.

Take for example, a pile of soft, fluffy mashed potatoes. If it came in a lovely shade of charcoal gray, you might not enjoy it as much as if it were white. (This brings new appreciation for Sam-I-Am and his *Green Eggs and Ham.*)

> **Tidbit**
>
> In high school, I worked at a small ice-cream parlor after school. Every month it held a contest: anyone who could guess the secret flavor would win a free gallon. It was almost always vanilla, colored purple or green or yellow stripped with orange. We had very few winners.

> **Hot Stuff**
>
> Certain foods turn gray through *oxidation*, a color change that occurs in the presence of oxygen. Cut and left exposed to air, foods such as potatoes, apples, artichokes, and bananas can quickly lose their appeal. Oxidation can be prevented, or at least slowed, by application of acid. Squirt the sliced food with lemon juice, or soak it in *acidulated* water (water with acid).

Combining the Senses

By now you've probably realized that it's impossible to enjoy food to its fullest extent without combining the senses. And if you pay attention to what you eat, you'll find that tastes seldom occur alone. They are almost always in combination.

Sweet and sour is a common pair, as in Chinese sweet-and-sour pork, or candies like Jolly Ranchers and lemon drops. Bitter and sweet are heavenly in chocolate and coffee. We feed our craving for salty and sour with pickled foods. And salty and sweet make terrific snacking with combinations like popcorn and candy at the movies, caramel corn, or honey-roasted nuts.

> **Tidbit**
>
> To experience the sweet and sour combination at its best, add a little raspberry vinegar to your favorite caramel sauce.

Once we begin to recognize flavor, we are compelled to explain it. Wine connoisseurs are renowned, and frequently mocked, for their creative flavor descriptions. The more one tries to explain flavor, the more adjectives from outside the realm of the kitchen are apt to be invoked. You will be hard pressed to find a description of flavor that does not include texture, but a few purely flavor-based adjectives are commonly used in combination to describe the way food tastes.

Meaty, earthy, and *woodsy* are often used to explain *umami.* Vegetables and herbs are commonly described as green, *herbaceous, grassy, piney, freshly mown hay, lawnmower bags,* and *football fields.* The unique flavors of spices are expressed with words like *musty, musky, fragrant, perfumey, floral, smoky,* and unfortunately, *spicy. Toasted, roasted, nutty, charred, carbonized,* and *caramelized* are used to describe flavor as well as explain cooking techniques.

Researchers have isolated hundreds of compounds that make food taste the way it does. When these compounds are concentrated, they become what are commonly known as *natural flavors.* Once the compound is understood, it can then be reproduced for *artificial flavors.* But although the compounds are chemically made of the same stuff, a banana jelly bean tastes different from an actual banana because more than one compound makes a banana taste the way it does. In addition, the jelly bean lacks the texture and color of the real thing.

> **Hot Stuff**
>
> Artificial flavoring can be used quite successfully to enhance a food's natural quality. But use a light hand, as too much can overpower a dish and mask the natural flavors. A common culprit is almond extract, used with too heavy a hand by many pastry chefs and bakers.

The Least You Need to Know

◆ Taste buds work throughout the mouth to detect the basic elements of taste.

◆ Flavor is determined by several senses working together.

◆ Tastes work best when used in combination.

Part 2

Flavor at Your Fingertips

What is *asafetida*, or *amchoor*, or *perilla?* Why do you need any of them? How do you get them?

From A to Z, in the following pages, you'll find a global array of flavor. Spices and herbs are listed with the cook in mind; included are flavor descriptions, common usage, and historical importance. Also included are a few recipes to whet your appetite and show you how a particular spice can be used. Some are common dishes from around the world, while others are more unusual flavor pairings meant to highlight the unique qualities of the ingredients. Try them and then venture out into your own culinary experiments.

Chapter 4

Spices and Herbs, A to Z

Now for the fun stuff: in this chapter is everything you ever wanted to know about spices and herbs. In addition to their culinary uses, I've given some basic botanical information, which will be of interest to gardening enthusiasts and those looking to find actual specimens of these plants.

In most cases, I've listed a botanical family for each entry. If it's been a while since your last science class, botanical families are a part of *scientific classification,* a system that categorizes species of organisms into increasingly specific groups. Order of classification is as follows:

Life

Domain   plants, animals, fungi, and protists fall into the domain called *Eukaryote*

Kingdom   plants are in the kingdom *plantae,* mushrooms and other fungus are in the kingdom *fungi,* and most algae is of the kingdom *protista*

Phylum/division   plant divisions are myriad and include those that are nonvascular, vascular, and seed bearing

Class   groups plants by physical characteristics

Order more descriptive than class

Family large, related groups of plants, like roses, citrus, palms, etc

Genus groups of similar plants, such as *thymus*, *cinnamomum*, and *rosmarinus*

Species one specific variation of a plant

For the purpose of this book, I feel that the *family* is the most interesting level of classification, because it indicates the more unusual plant relationships.

Algae and seaweed classification is more difficult because these organisms fall somewhere in between plants and animals. The kingdom *protista* has been established for such plants and animals. They share the characteristic of complex cell or cells with a membrane bound nucleus.

Individual *species* are also listed throughout the text when specific plant variations are discussed. This nomenclature is useful when ordering plants from nurseries and through the Internet.

Also listed, when necessary, are pseudonyms. In some cases, I listed only the most common names because there were so many. If you're having trouble locating a certain spice or herb, try one of its aliases.

As you read through this section, I urge you to jot down the spices and herbs you find interesting. Be adventurous, and visit a specialty spice market, or go online to order something new, just for fun. There's a big world of flavor out there just waiting for you to take a bite!

Achiote

See Annatto.

Agar

A member of the botanical family *gelidiaceae*

(Algae is technically neither plant nor animal.)

Also known as *agar-agar, kanten,* and *Japanese gelatin*

Agar is a tasteless thickener made from a type of red algae (*gelidium*). After the marine plant is harvested, it's dried and bleached in the sun. Next it goes through a series of stages—boiling, crushing, freezing, and thawing—all designed to eliminate impurities and extract the pure gum.

Agar is used in much the same manner as gelatin. The product is dissolved in hot water, added to recipes, and chilled to set. It absorbs nearly three times its volume of water, and for that reason has its place in the halls of fad diets, especially in Japan, where kanten tea is a hot item for the overweight.

Agar is used in many desserts and sweets throughout Asia and in beer brewing as a clarifying agent. The gums extracted from marine vegetation (called *alginates*) make frequent appearances on the labels of processed food as thickeners, emulsifiers, and stabilizers. Like agar, the other alginates, which include carrgeenan and furcellaran, are used widely in the food industry. Agar is the only one frequently used by home and restaurant cooks.

Agar is available in better supermarkets and most Asian grocery stores. It comes as sticks of dried seaweed or in powdered form.

Agave

A member of the botanical family *agavaceae*

Also known as *century plant, American aloe,* and *maguey*

This succulent plant (*agave americana*), a relative of yucca and aloe, is native to Mexico and grows abundantly there, as well as areas of the southwestern United States. It has large, long, thick leaves with spiny sharp edges that taper to a sharp point. The leaves sprout out from the root like a green fountain. After a decade of development, the flower majestically sprouts like a tree from the center just once during the plant's life, hence its pseudonym, century plant. The plant is poisonous if eaten raw, but sweet fruit, sap, or nectar is extracted from the stem.

Native tribes used this sap to make a ceremonial fermented drink called *pulque*. Pulque is still enjoyed in Mexico, but because it has a short shelf life, it's rarely seen outside that country. Some canned versions see limited import into the United States, but most agree that pulque is best enjoyed fresh in pulqueria cantinas.

The sap from agave is also distilled into a spirit known in Mexico as *Mescal.* Mescal is any distillation of agave that is not tequila. To be called tequila, the juice must come from the *blue agave* (*agave tequilana*) and be produced under strict guidelines in specific regions surrounding the town of Tequila in the central western state of Jalisco.

Agave nectar is used as a sweetener and sugar substitute. It is $1^1/_2$ times sweeter than cane sugar or honey, but it has a much lower glycemic index, which means it's absorbed more slowly into the bloodstream. This prevents it from raising blood sugar levels significantly, eliminating the highs and lows associated with sugar intake. For this reason, it's favored among those with diabetes and hyperglycemia.

Creative chefs use agave nectar anywhere sugar or honey will go: barbecue sauces, marinades, baked goods, etc. It adds a distinctive sweet flavor, reminiscent of—you guessed it—tequila.

Agave nectar is available through Internet sources (rawagave.com, agavenectar.com) and at health food stores.

Agave Vinaigrette

Don't limit this dressing to your salad bowl. Try it on grilled seafood and poultry, too.

3 TB. agave nectar
1 clove garlic, minced
½ tsp. sea salt
¼ tsp. fresh ground black pepper
Zest and juice of 1 Mexican lime
2 TB. fresh cilantro, minced
¼ cup champagne vinegar
1 cup olive oil
6 cups loosely packed fresh salad greens (baby mixed greens, spinach, halved cherry tomatoes, and diced avocado)
1 cup fried flour or corn tortilla strips
½ cup crumbled cotija cheese

1. Whisk together agave nectar, garlic, sea salt, pepper, lime zest and juice, cilantro, vinegar, and olive oil in a large bowl, or combine in a jar with a tight-fitting lid and shake.

2. Pour vinaigrette over salad greens, toss, and top with tortilla strips and crumbled cotija.

Aji-No-Moto

See MSG.

Ajowan

A member of the botanical family *umbelliferae* (parsley)

Also known as *ajwain*, *carum*, *Ethiopian cumin*, and *bishop's weed*

Native to India and North Africa, the ajowan plant (*trachyspermum ammi*) is a thin plant with leaves like carrot tops and white tufts of flowers that look like Queen Anne's lace. The tiny seeds look striped upon close inspection, much like fennel seeds, and they have a hairlike tail similar to anise.

The flavor of the ajowan seed is a little like thyme, as it contains the same aromatic compound thymol. But it's more complex, reminiscent of caraway, celery seed, and cumin.

The seed is common in Indian cuisine, often finding its way into starchy foods like breads, legumes, and vegetable dishes. It's an important flavor element in West African dishes as well, especially groundnut soup, and it is included in several of the region's traditional spice blends, including *kala masla* and *berbere* (see Appendix B).

Look for ajowan in Indian markets or online (nirmalaskitchen.com).

Aloo Paratha Bread

This stuffed Indian bread is a meal in itself.

2 cups whole-wheat flour
1 tsp. salt
½ to 1 cup cold water
½ cup ghee or vegetable oil
1 small onion, chopped
1 green chile pepper, minced
1 tsp. coriander seeds, crushed
1 tsp. ajowan seeds, crushed
5 small red new potatoes, boiled
1 tsp. cilantro, chopped

1. In a small bowl, combine flour and salt. Slowly stir in water to form a firm dough. Knead dough for 2 minutes, cover, and let rest for 30 minutes.

2. Heat 2 tablespoons ghee in a large sauté pan over high heat. Add onion, cook until golden. Add chile pepper, coriander seeds, and ajowan seeds, and fry briefly to toast. Remove from heat and stir in potatoes and cilantro. Set aside to cool.

3. Divide dough into 6 portions and form into balls. Pat each ball into a flat disc and fill with 1 or 2 tablespoons potato filling. Pinch dough closed around filling, and roll out into flat circle on a floured work surface, seam side down. Repeat with remaining dough.

4. Fry stuffed dough circles in 1 or 2 tablespoons ghee until golden brown on each side.

Allspice

A member of the botanical family *myrtaceae* (myrtle)

Also known as *Jamaican pepper* and *pimento*

This evergreen member of the myrtle family (*pimenta dioica*) grows in tropical and subtropical regions of South America and the West Indies. It has tough, thick leaves and small white clumps of tiny flowers that give way to dark purple berries. The berries are picked green and dried off the tree. Once dried, they resemble black pepper, which is why, upon discovery of this spice in Jamaica, Christopher Columbus named it *Jamaican Pepper*. Back in Europe, it was dubbed *pimento*.

The most sought-after allspice is Jamaican, but it is grown in other tropical regions as well, including Mexico, Guatemala, and Honduras.

Despite its name, allspice is not a blend of all the spices, although its flavor does closely resemble a combination of clove, cinnamon, nutmeg, and pepper.

Because of its similarity to those spices, allspice is frequently used in sweet, spicy baking. Its flavor is particularly suited to firm but mild root vegetables and squashes, like beets, parsnips, butternut, and acorn squash. It adds a nice flavor to peas and leafy greens and is commonly used much like nutmeg is in classic egg, cheese, and starch dishes. Allspice makes frequent appearances in sauces and marinades, most famously *Jerk* (see Appendix B).

Ground or powdered allspice is readily available, while whole allspice berries are available in larger supermarkets.

Almond

A member of the botanical family rosaceae (rose)

Although usually considered a nut, this fruit pit is a seed and an important flavoring worldwide. A native tree of Asia, almonds are now cultivated mainly in California, Spain, and Italy.

Two types of almonds are used in food production. Sweet almonds (*prunus dulcius*) can be eaten out of hand and are used in most recipes. Bitter almonds (*prunus dulcius amara*) have a specific, unique flavor used in the preparation of amaretto liqueur and almond extract. A similar flavor is extracted from apricot and peach pits and is often used in conjunction with or in place of bitter almonds.

Sweet almonds are available in multiple forms, including whole, skin on, blanched, toasted, slivered, sliced, chopped, and ground into fine almond meal and almond flour. Bitter almonds take a bit more effort to track down but are usually available at Indian or Middle Eastern Markets or online (bitteralmond.com). Bitter almonds contain a high percentage of hydrocyanic acid, which, while poisonous, is easily cooked out. Almonds contain a large amount of oil and are best refrigerated if not used right away to prevent rancidity.

Alum

Potassium aluminum sulfate

This mysterious white powder is actually powdered crystals of a salt of sulfuric acid. Alum is found in many industrial applications, including use as a dye fixative and as a fire retardant, but home cooks have relied on it for years as a crisping agent for pickling. Today, while most pickled vegetable recipes rely on refrigeration as a crisper and preservative, many pickling aficionados still add alum for the extra edge, especially during county fair time.

Alum is also an astringent and can be found in many old home remedies for relief of canker sores, to stop bleeding of small cuts, and as a deodorant. It's used in some home recipes for play dough, slowing down the growth of bacteria, and making it taste so bad that even paste-loving kids won't eat it.

Although alum is no longer a pantry staple, you can still find it in the spice aisle, as enterprising homemakers rely on it to this day.

Amaranth

A member of the botanical family *amaranthaceae* (pigweed)

Also known as *kiwicha*, *Chinese spinach*, and *bayam*

Amaranth (*amaranthus cruentis*) is a showy plant, with bushy broad leaves and a feathery fountain of tiny pink, red, and purple flowers. Several species are grown for specific uses, including the edible seeds, the edible leaves, dye extracted from the flowers, and their beauty in the garden.

The tiny tan and black amaranth seed contains complete protein, and for that reason, it was a staple food of the Incas, Aztecs, and Mayans. Its cultivation stopped when the Spanish arrived in the new world, but amaranth has experienced renewed popularity in recent years because of its nutritional value, especially among vegetarians.

The amaranth seed is used in a multitude of ways. It's ground to a flour and added to breads and pasta. The grain itself contains no gluten, but it adds an interesting nutty flavor when added to wheat flour. It can be used alone in recipes for crackers and flatbreads and makes good pancakes, similar in flavor to buckwheat. The seeds can be eaten as a porridge, boiled like rice with $1^1/_2$ times its volume in water. Add other herbs, vegetables, and nuts for an interesting pilaf.

The grains can also be popped like popcorn for a completely different flavor and texture. These tiny airy grains are commonly mixed with honey or syrup to create nutritious confections—called *alegria* in Mexico and *laddoos* in India—similar to Rice Krispy treats.

The greens are eaten like spinach throughout Asia, Mexico, and Peru. Amaranth sprouts are added to salads or sandwiches.

Amaranth seeds are available in most health food stores. For the leaves, look to local farmers' markets, or try to grow your own (naturehills.com).

Amchoor

A member of the botanical family *anacardiaceae* (cashew)

Also known as *mango powder* and *amchur*

Amchoor is a yellow-green powder made from mangos (*magifera*) that are picked green, dried in the sun, and ground to a powder. It's a common ingredient in Northern India and Nepal, used frequently in spice blends, including *Chaat Masala* (see Appendix B).

Amchoor has a very tart, sour-apple flavor and is used like lemon or lime juice to awaken flavors of a dish. It contains citric acid and proteolytic enzymes (enzymes that break down protein), which not only add flavor, but act as a meat tenderizer.

Amchoor is available whole or powdered in Indian markets and online (thespicebazaar.com).

Sweet Fruit Chutney

The sweet tanginess of this dish is the perfect antidote to fiery curry.

2 TB. amchoor powder

1 tsp. cumin

1 tsp. red chile powder

½ tsp. sea salt

¼ cup sugar

2 TB. fresh ginger, grated

2 TB. fresh cilantro, chopped

4 bananas, diced

1 mango, diced

1 papaya, diced

½ cup shredded coconut

½ cup golden raisins

1. In a large bowl, combine amchoor powder, cumin, red chile powder, sea salt, and sugar. Mix well, and add ginger and cilantro. Add bananas, mango, papaya, coconut, and raisins, and toss to coat.

2. Serve with spicy curries and warm flatbread.

Ammonia Bicarbonate

Also known as *hartshorn, baking ammonia,* and *carbonate of ammonia*

Ammonia bicarbonate was commonly used as a leavener before the advent of baking soda. It was used in many heavily spiced recipes because it left behind a slight ammonia flavor that's easily masked by spices.

Like baking powder, ammonia bicarbonate releases carbon dioxide **A** when moistened and heated. The name *hartshorn* came from one early form of processing, when it was extracted from a distillation of hoofs and horns. Old Scandinavian recipes still call for hartshorn. It's not readily available, although some pharmacies may carry a crystalline version, which must be ground before using.

An equal amount of baking powder can be substituted.

Ancho

See Appendix C.

Anaheim

See Appendix C.

Angelica

> A member of the botanical family *umbelliferae* (parsley)
>
> Also known as *angel's root* and *wild celery*

Native to subarctic regions—including Russia, Northern Europe, Scandinavia, Iceland, and northern parts of North America—this giant herb (*angelica archangelica*) has large jagged-edged leaves that grow in groups of three. The tall, hollow stalk has red-tinged celerylike ridges and can grow as high as 6 feet tall. The tiny yellow-green flowers grow in pom-pom clusters.

Many cultures used angelica medicinally and spiritually throughout history. It was tacked above doorways to ward off plague, carried as defense against evil spirits and witchcraft, and smoked by Native Americans as a cure for respiratory ailments. Best of all, it's believed to be a panacea, and as such is protected by the Archangel Michael.

The subtle licorice-anise-sage flavor of angelica is enjoyed in several forms. The stalks are eaten as a vegetable in Scandinavian cuisines, and the leaves and seeds (see *Golpar*) are found in fish, meat, and stew preparations. Angelica seeds are among the many herbs used to flavor vermouth, chartreuse, and gin. The sweet root is used in jellies, fruit sauces, and potpourri. But by far the most common application of angelica is the candied stem.

The celerylike stalk is candied, often artificially colored green, and used by pastry chefs as a decorative element or incorporated into recipes with other dried and candied fruits. Angelica is naturally sweet, but candied angelica has extra sugar added, masking much of the natural herb's delicate flavor.

You can find angelica plants at better nurseries or online (mountainvalleygrowers.com). Candied angelica is imported from France; many spice companies carry it (herbies.com.au).

Angelica can be stored in syrup, or drained, coated with granulated sugar, and air dried. Store dried, sugared angelica in an airtight container at room temperature. Save the syrup for sweetening your iced tea.

Candied Angelica

Store-bought candied angelica is too sugary for me. This version lets the flavor shine through.

4 cups sugar

4 cups water

2 or 3 cups angelica stems, peeled, blanched, and cut into 1-in. segments

1. In a large saucepan, combine sugar and water and bring to a boil. At the boil, add angelica and reduce heat to low.

2. Cook at barely a simmer for 30 to 60 minutes until stems are tender and translucent. Remove from heat and cool completely.

Anise

A member of the botanical family *umbelliferae* (parsley)

Anise refers to an annual flowering herb (*pimpinella anisum*) grown mainly for its seeds. Growing about 20 inches high, the leaves at the base of the plant look similar to cilantro, with the leaves at the top looking more like dill. White flowers produce a distinctive ridged seed with a small curly tail.

Anise was well-known to the ancient Romans, who used it to flavor hardtack carried by soldiers and sailors, a food similar to today's Italian biscotti, the twice-baked cookie, which is so hard it is meant to be dipped in *vin santo* or coffee.

The anise seed tastes like light licorice, but is sweeter and more delicate than fennel or licorice root. It's used most famously in several liqueurs, including its Italian namesake Anisette, Sambuca, Middle Eastern Arak, Greek Ouzo, and French Pastis. It also appears in many candies and chocolates. Lighter meats like fish and poultry are enhanced by its delicate but distinct flavors, and it shows up in several soups and stews throughout the Pyrenees region of France.

The anise seed is well loved in India as a digestive aid. Brightly colored, sugar-coated seeds of anise, fennel, and sesame called *mukhwas* are commonly served after meals to soothe the tongue and tummy after spicy meals—and to freshen breath.

You can find anise seed and powder at any well-stocked market. Specialty stores, especially pastry suppliers, may also carry anise extract or oil. Sometimes fennel bulb is mislabeled *sweet anise* in the produce department of your grocery store. Don't be fooled.

Annatto

A member of the botanical family *bixaceae* (annatto)

Also known as *achiote*

The achiote tree or shrub (*bixa orellana*), native to South America and the Caribbean, has heart-shape leaves and a spiny heart-shape seed pod that contains the annatto seed. The red pulp and tiny red seeds have been used historically as paint and dye. It's currently used as a colorant in many commercially prepared foods, including cheese, butter, candy, and smoked fish.

Annatto seed has a subtle bay-juniper flavor that's favored in meat dishes throughout South America and the Pacific. Philippine cuisine takes full advantage of the annatto seed, incorporating it into all kinds of stews, sauces, and fried foods.

The seeds themselves are very hard, and when ground, still tend to add a touch of grit to a recipe. The most efficient method of incorporating annatto seeds is to first cook them in oil, strain out the seeds, and use the oil. Another way to incorporate annatto is to use a commercially prepared paste, called *achiote paste*.

Both the seeds and the paste can be found easily in Latin American markets or in the ethnic aisle of better supermarkets.

Annatto Chicken

This dish can be frightening to those who don't enjoy spicy heat. But tell them to relax. It's more *spiced* than *spicy*.

1 cup olive oil
½ cup annatto seeds
4 cloves garlic, minced
1 yellow onion, diced
1 TB. fresh oregano, chopped
1 tsp. cumin seeds, crushed
1 tsp. whole allspice, crushed
2 bay leaves, crushed
1 tsp. peppercorns, crushed
Zest and juice of 1 large orange
Zest and juice of 1 lime
¼ cup white wine vinegar
1 (4- or 5-lb.) chicken, cut into serving pieces and rinsed with water

1. In a small saucepan over low heat, combine oil and annatto seeds and cook, stirring, until oil is red and aromatic, about 10 minutes. Cool and strain off and discard seeds.

2. In a large bowl, combine annatto oil with garlic, onion, oregano, cumin, allspice, bay leaves, peppercorns, orange zest and juice, lime zest and juice, and vinegar. Stir well to combine.

3. Put rinsed chicken pieces into a large plastic zipper bag. Pour in marinade and seal the bag. Massage marinade into meat and refrigerate for 4 to 6 hours. Grill or sauté chicken over low heat until the skin is crispy and the internal temperature reaches 180°F, about 10 minutes per side.

Variation: You could also roast the chicken at 400°F for 45 to 60 minutes.

Aonori

From the botanical family *ulvales*

(Algae is technically neither a plant nor an animal.)

Also known as *green nori*

Aonori is a Japanese product made from green algae (*monostroma* and *enteromorpha*). It is farmed in bays around Japan, harvested, dried, and ground into a fine, bright-green powder.

High in calcium, iron, and protein, aonori is used as a flavoring and garnish in everyday dishes such as soup, rice, noodles, and tempura.

Find powdered and traditional flaked and paper forms of aonori in Japanese markets or online (importfood.com).

Arrowroot

From the botanical family *marantaceae*

Also known as the *obedience plant*

This perennial plant (*maranta arundinaceae*), native to the West Indies, shoots stalks up as high as 5 feet. But it's the *rhizome* that contains the precious starch so important to the cuisines of Southeast Asia.

According to legend, the roots were pounded, and the starchy pulp was used to extract the toxins from poisoned-arrow wounds.

Chefspeak

Although often confused with a root, a **rhizome** is actually a bulbous, underground stem that grows horizontally at the soil surface.

Today, the flavorless white powder is a thickening agent preferred in lighter sauces that are meant to stay clear. Unlike flour or cornstarch, arrowroot requires no additional cooking or boiling time to eliminate a starchy flavor, nor does it take on an opaque, cloudy appearance.

Arrowroot is not, however, an all-purpose starch replacement. Overheating arrowroot destroys its thickening power. It can also take on a slimy consistency when used with dairy products. It's best to add arrowroot to a sauce at the end of cooking, when a little more body and texture is desired.

Arrowroot is available in larger supermarkets and most health food stores.

Asafetida

A member of the botanical family *umbelliferae* (parsley)

Also known as *asefoetida* and *devil's dung*

Foetida is Latin for "foul-smelling," which makes one wonder who discovered asafetida and why they decided to put it in their mouth. Asafetida is the dried sap of a giant fennel plant (*ferula asafetida*). It has a distinct, off-putting, sulphurous smell, but once gently heated, it imparts a pleasantly distinctive garlicy essence.

Asafetida is an integral component of many forms of Indian *dal* (legumes), South Indian *Sambar Podi* (see Appendix B), and the ubiquitous Worcestershire sauce.

The dried sap or resin is very hard and, thus, difficult to grind. It must be fried in hot oil to release its flavors. For asafetida first-timers, buy it in Middle Eastern and Indian Markets in prepared powder form, which usually includes some proportion of starch. Keep asafetida powder tightly sealed, or the rest of the spices in the pantry can take on its menacing odor.

Toasted Rice Pilaf

The spices in this dish makes it special, but it's the toasting of the rice before the liquid is added that provides a deep, rich, nutty flavor.

¼ cup vegetable oil
1 yellow onion, diced
2 cloves garlic, minced
1 sweet red pepper, diced
½ tsp. mustard seed, crushed
½ tsp. cumin seed, crushed
½ tsp. coriander seed, crushed
1 tsp. fresh ginger, grated
1 tsp. asafetida powder
2 curry leaves
2 cups basmati rice
1 cup golden raisins
1 cup sliced almonds
4 cups water
¼ cup chopped cilantro

1. In a large, wide-bottomed sauté pan or soup pot, heat vegetable oil. Add onion, garlic, and sweet red pepper, and sauté until translucent.

2. Add mustard seed, cumin seed, coriander seed, ginger, asafetida powder, curry leaves, and rice, and stir to coat with oil. Toast over high heat until rice begins to turn golden brown and spices become fragrant.

3. Add raisins, almonds, and water, and bring to a boil. At the boil, turn heat down to a bare simmer, cover, and cook for 20 minutes or until water is absorbed and rice is tender.

4. Serve topped with chopped cilantro.

Baking Powder

This leavener is not technically a spice, but it does appear on every spice shelf, so it's worth a quick mention. First marketed in the 1860s, baking powder is a mixture of *bicarbonate of soda* and an acidic salt, such as cream of tartar or calcium phosphate, with some starch thrown in for easy blending.

When baking powder is mixed into a recipe, it reacts with the moisture of the batter and the heat of the oven to produce carbon dioxide. The gas builds up and raises the product. Double-acting baking powder begins this process when moistened but holds a portion of the reaction until heat is applied. The original baking powder, single-acting baking powder, releases all the carbon dioxide with moisture and must, therefore, be baked immediately upon mixing.

Baking Soda

Bicarbonate of soda

This chemical compound is created when ammonia is used to separate the sodium (Na) from the chloride (Cl) of salt (NaCl) in the presence of carbon dioxide and water. When added to acid, it releases carbon dioxide gas. (Remember the papier-mâché volcano trick from elementary school science class?) When mixed into batters with acidic ingredients like vinegar, sour cream, or buttermilk, the gas accumulates and leavens the product.

Baking soda is also used in some applications to increase alkali in highly acidic foods. This increased alkali preserves the color of some fruits vegetables.

Basil

A member of the botanical family *labiatae* (mint)

Also known as *sweet basil* and *holy basil*

A native of India, basil *(ocimum basilicum)* spread to Asia and Egypt as early as 2000 B.C.E. It moved up through Europe with the help of the Romans and came to the New World with the colonists. Basil is a sacred plant in India, a symbol of love, faithfulness, and eternal life. It is often associated with the scorpion, thought to protect against them in some cultures and attract them in others. Early Christians believe basil grew at the sight of the Crucifixion and is, therefore, found on the altar and in the Holy Water at the Greek Orthodox Church.

This short plant, which can be grown as a perennial in hot climates, is favored for its silky, shiny, juicy, fragrant leaves. There are many varieties, including those with smooth green leaves, serrated-edged leaves, curly lettuce leaves, purple-tinged leaves, and very dark purple leaves. Flowers shoot up in purple or white spikes and are as fragrant as the leaves.

Basil leaves are strong and oily when fresh, with a gingery, licorice flavor. When dried, basil takes on the minty flavor of its plant family. To preserve the fresh flavor of basil, store it frozen as blanched leaves or purées, or pack the fresh leaves in salt. Interesting hybrids are available, and the flavors can be surmised from the names, such as pineapple basil, lemon basil, and cinnamon basil.

Although most often associated with Mediterranean cuisines, basil is also a vital ingredient in foods from Thailand and Vietnam. The pungent aroma complements all kinds of food, including red meat, seafood, poultry, vegetables, eggs, cheeses, and many different berries and stone fruits.

Dried basil is readily available in most markets. Better supermarkets and most farmers' markets carry fresh basil, especially throughout the summer. Basil is also an easy plant to grow in the garden or on the kitchen windowsill.

Bay

A member of the botanical family *lauraceae* (laurel)

Also known as *bay laurel, sweet bay, roman laurel,* and *Turkish bay*

This evergreen tree (*laurus nobilis*) is native to the Mediterranean but thrives wherever the climate is similar. It was dedicated to Apollo, the god of music and poetry, and garlands of laurel were given as prizes—hence *poet laureate* and *baccalaureate*. It grows up to 30 feet high and produces creamy little flowers and blackberries. But it's the leaves that are prized above all.

About 3 inches long, thick and shiny, the leaves are used dry or fresh with meats, fish, vegetables, stews, soups, pâtés, marinades, and even fruits. The subtle pine-camphor aroma is slightly bitter when fresh but takes on a sweetness as it dries.

Indian Bay (*cinnamomum tamala*) is also known as cinnamon leaf and has a decidedly cinnamon flavor. It's used extensively in *kormas* and curries. California Bay (*umbellularia californica*) is a more potent, mentholated variety, and is best when not overcooked. Indonesian Bay (*Eugenia polyantha*) is actually in the myrtle family and has the subtle essence of anise.

Common bay leaves are available dried at most markets. Looking for specific Turkish or California bay may require a trip online (savoryspiceshop.com). You can find Indian Bay at Indian markets, but Indonesian is a little trickier to find—unless you live near an Indonesian community.

Chefspeak

A **korma** is a mild meat or vegetable curry, usually made with nuts, coconut milk, yogurt, or cream.

Hot Stuff

Many people prefer to remove the bay leaves from a dish before serving, but I like the look of them. They don't hurt and won't make anyone ill, so I leave them in for beauty and aroma. People can eat around them!

Warm Winter Compote

This recipe calls for the *bosc* variety of pear, the very pear-shape pears with brownish skin and firm flesh. They hold their shape well for prolonged cooking, which makes them ideal here. If you can't find them, any pear will do, as will, for that matter, apples.

2 pt. dried black mission figs
4 bosc pears, peeled, cored, and sliced
1 cup pomegranate seeds
1 vanilla bean, split
1 cinnamon stick, crushed
3 bay leaves, crushed
Zest and juice of 1 lemon
1 TB. honey
3 cups apple juice
1 cup water

1. Trim fig stems, cut figs in half, and place in a medium sauce-pan. Add pears, pomegranate seeds, vanilla bean, cinnamon stick, bay leaves, lemon zest and juice, honey, apple juice, and water, and set over high heat.

2. At the boil, reduce heat to a bare simmer and cook for 30 minutes. Remove from heat and cool. Spoon warm over vanilla ice cream or gingerbread.

Bear's Garlic

A member of the botanical family *alliaceae* (onion)

Also known as *ramsons* and *wood garlic*

Some believe this wild onion (*alium ursinum*) is the first food bears eat upon awaking from hibernation. It grows in swampy, shady woodlands throughout Central Europe and is used in many local cuisines. It has broad, short green leaves, and sprouts into an onion stalk with a pom-pom of white star-shaped flowers.

The young leaves of this wild onion have a delicate chive flavor and are collected before the plant flowers to flavor salads, cheese, soups, and sauces. The flowers themselves have a delicate onion flavor and can be scattered into salads. Bear's garlic is currently the hot, trendy ingredient sought by European foodies.

Bear's garlic is not cultivated in the United States, but if you have a shady, woodsy yard, and a green thumb, you can give it a shot (b-and-t-world-seeds.com).

Benne Seed

See Sesame Seed.

Bergamot

A member of the botanical family *labiatae* (mint)

Also known as *red bergamot, Oswego tea, Indian plume,* and *bee balm*

You can find several varieties of this tall perennial (*monarda didyma*), native to North America. The Oswego Indians of western New York dried and steeped the leaves into tea, and colonists drank it when English tea was politically incorrect. Early settlers used it to relieve sore throats and inhaled fumes to treat colds.

The fat, jagged leaves have a reddish tinge, and its shaggy red pom-pom flower makes it a favorite of ornamental gardeners. The leaves have a bright citrus flavor and are mixed fresh into salads, fruits, and drinks.

Bergamot is not a common market item, but it's easily grown, as many nurseries carry it or can order it (wellsweep.com).

Hot Stuff

Do not confuse bergamot with *orange bergamot* (*citrus aurantium bergamia*), a hybrid of the Seville orange and grapefruit. The distinct flavor of Earl Grey tea comes from the oil of the orange bergamot.

Bitter Almond

See Almond.

Black Cardamom

See Cardamom.

Black Mustard

See Mustard.

Black Onion Seed

See Nigella.

Blue Fenugreek

See Fenugreek.

Boldo

A member of the botanical family *monimiaceae*

Also known as *boldina leaf*

This aromatic evergreen tree (*peumus boldus*) is native to the Andes, and its leaves are used extensively in the cuisines of Chile and Argentina. It has been used by the native tribes of the Andes as an all-purpose elixir, curing everything from the common cold to gallbladder and liver disease. It's still frequently steeped into a tea to calm an upset stomach.

Similar in appearance to its cousin, bay laurel, boldo is has a similar flavor, with a hint of peppery cinnamon. Use it wherever you would bay leaf, including roasted and stewed meats, vegetables, soups, and stews.

If you live in Brazil, you'll find boldo in every market. If not, try the Internet (mountainroseherbs.com).

Borage

A member of the botanical family *boraginaceae*

Also known as *star flower*

Native of Syria, this small annual plant (*borago officinalis*) has a fuzzy stem and leaves and small blue flowers with five-pointed petals, like a star.

Like many herbs, borage made its way to Europe via the Romans, who considered it a source of courage. Early colonists brought it to North America. Besides its culinary applications, the herb was used to improve mood and drive out melancholy. It's still considered a good herbal remedy for PMS. Borage is rich in potassium and calcium and has been shown to stimulate adrenal glands.

The leaves and young buds have a cool, cucumberlike flavor that's well suited to salads and herb sauces. The flowers, which have a subtle honey essence, are often candied and used as pastry decoration, frozen in ice cubes, or steeped and pounded into refreshing beverages. Large leaves are eaten like spinach, fresh, sautéed, or added to vegetable dishes. The Germans use it in a well-known green sauce mixed with parsley, chives, chervil, sorrel, yogurt, and cream cheese, and served with boiled eggs and potatoes.

Borage is available at many farmers markets in the spring, and seeds can be found at most nurseries (snowseedco.com).

Burnet

A member of the botanical family *rosacea* (rose)

Also known as *salad burnet*

This hearty perennial is native to the Mediterranean. Its botanical name, *sanguisorba officinalis*, means "to absorb blood," and historically, its astringent properties were thought to reduce bleeding. Soldiers going into battle drank tea infused with burnet to improve their chances of survival.

Burnet was common in formal herb gardens throughout England and is used extensively as a salad green throughout Europe. Colonists brought it to North America, where its delicate foliage and tiny red blossoms are prized more as ornamental than culinary.

As its pseudonym indicates, burnet is terrific on salads. Its young tender, lacy leaves have a light, pleasant cucumber flavor. Pick the leaves young, as they tend to get bitter with age. Add them not only to salads, but to soups, cool drinks, or butter or mix into eggs and cheese.

This crop appears at trendier farmers markets, but your best bet is to grow your own, from plants (mulberrycreek.com) or seeds (greenchronicle.com).

Herb Cooler

Serve this thirst-quencher over ice, with some borage flowers floating on top.

¼ cup chopped fresh burnet
2 TB. chopped fresh peppermint
Zest and juice of 1 lemon
Zest and juice of 1 orange
2 TB. honey
1 (1-in.) chunk fresh ginger root
4 cups boiling water
6 cups cold water
1 handful borage flowers

1. In a large heatproof bowl, combine burnet, peppermint, lemon zest and juice, orange zest and juice, honey, and ginger. Pour boiling water over and steep for 30 minutes, stirring occasionally.

2. Strain into a serving pitcher, add cold water, stir, and top with borage flowers before serving.

Cajun Spice

See Appendix B.

Caper

A member of the botanical family *capparidaceae*

Also known as *caperberry*

Native of the Mediterranean, capers come from a small biennial bush (*capparis sipinosa*) with trailing prickly stems and thin, glossy leaves. If allowed to blossom, the flowers are tiny purple and white. But the olive-green buds are harvested before they bloom, dried, and pickled in a salt and vinegar brine or packed in salt.

The tangy flavor of capers is a common accompaniment to seafood. It appears in sauces, tomato dishes, eggs, as garnish, and even in cocktails. Use care when adding capers to a recipe. Because they are cured in salt, they add salt to whatever recipe they go into. Rinsing them before use reduces this effect, and lets more of the sharp, acidic caper flavor emerge.

You can find capers in the same grocery store aisle as pickles and olives.

Caraway

A member of the botanical family *umbelliferae* (parsley)

This ancient herb (*carum caravi*) has been found among Neolithic ruins of Europe, and in the Middle Ages, it was known as a useful anti-gas remedy.

The leaves of this biennial plant look like carrot leaves at the base and then become thin and feathery toward the top as it flowers in tufts of tiny white blossoms. The stems and leaves have a mild flavor similar to parsley. The roots have a sweet, parsnip flavor and can be cooked and eaten in a similar manner—boiled or fried. It's the seeds, however, that get the most attention.

In the west, caraway seeds are most associated with breads, notably rye bread. Those who find rye bread disagreeable blame the caraway. The flavor is heady, like a strong combination of thyme and dill. It's found in all kinds of foods throughout northern Europe and Scandinavia, paired often with cabbage and root vegetables, meats, cheeses, and even fruits. Caraway is also a major component of *aquavit*, a herbal Scandinavian distilled liquor.

Apples, Fennel, and Onions with Caraway

This dish make a terrific accompaniment to roasted poultry, pork, or sausage.

4 TB. butter
1 TB. caraway seed, crushed
1 yellow onion, sliced thin
1 fennel bulb, sliced thin
2 fuji apples, peeled, cored, and sliced thin
1 cup dry white wine
1 tsp. sea salt

1. In a large sauté pan, melt butter over high heat. Add caraway seed and toast until fragrant, 1 or 2 minutes. Add onion and sauté until translucent. Add fennel and apples, and continue sautéing over high heat until everything is golden brown and caramelized.

2. Deglaze with white wine, and cook until liquid is evaporated. Remove from heat, add salt, and serve warm.

Cardamom

A member of the botanical family *zingiberaceae* (ginger)

An Asian shrub in the ginger family, cardamom (*elettaria cardamomum*) grows long, pointed leaves off a large stem, similar to tulips or iris. Its tropical flower makes way for plump seed pods that contain the pungent, oil-rich cardamom seeds. The pods are picked by hand when green and dried in the sun. They're sold green, which are not processed beyond natural drying, and white, which are treated with sulfur dioxide to mute the flavors.

Black cardamom (*afromomum subulatun*) has a completely different smoky, peppery quality because it's dried over open, smoky flames. It can hold up well to, and is preferred for, heavier, spicier dishes than the green or white pods. That said, there's no need to run to the store for black if all you've got is green.

Cardamom is popular in India, where it's a common ingredient in curries and rice dishes. Scandinavian and Bavarian chefs know cardamom well and take advantage of its sweet overtones in fruits, breads, and pastries. It's also a key ingredient in strong, cloyingly sweet Turkish coffee.

Ground cardamom is widely available, and white pods can be found in better markets. Green and black may take a little more time to track down (savoryspiceshop.com).

Turkish Coffee Cookies

These cookies are sweet and exotic and make a terrific accompaniment to coffee, tea, or a tall glass of milk.

2⅓ cups all-purpose flour

¾ tsp. baking powder

¼ tsp. salt

2 sticks butter

2 tsp. freshly ground cardamom

2 TB. instant powdered espresso

3⅔ cups sugar

1 TB. vanilla extract

1 egg

1 TB. milk

2 TB. *cinnamon sugar*

1. Preheat the oven to 350°F. Line 2 baking sheets with parchment paper.

2. Sift together flour, baking powder, and salt, and set aside.

3. In a large bowl and using a sturdy spoon or an electric mixer, cream butter, cardamom, powdered espresso, and sugar until free of lumps. Add vanilla extract, egg, and milk. Slowly add sifted ingredients and mix well to fully incorporate. Chill dough for 30 minutes.

4. Roll out chilled cookie dough on a floured surface to ¼ inch thick. Cut out cookies with a floured cookie cutter and place cookies on lined baking sheets 1 inch apart. Sprinkle each cookie lightly with cinnamon sugar and bake at 350° for 10 to 12 minutes or until golden brown on the edges. Cool for 5 minutes before removing from baking sheets.

Chefspeak

Cinnamon sugar is simply a mixture of granulated sugar and ground cinnamon. I prefer mine in a 2:1 ratio (2 parts sugar to 1 part cinnamon).

Cassava

A member of the botanical family *euphorbiaceae*

Also known as *yuca* and *manioc*

A woody annual shrub in the spurge family, cassava (*manihot esculenta*) is cultivated for its root. The plant is native to South America but is now grown and eaten all over the world. It is a staple food throughout Africa, where it's grated or pounded, mixed with water, and cooked to a paste. India and Indonesia also consider it an important food, where it's eaten like a potato—boiled, fried, mashed, and added to recipes like dumplings, stews, and soups. In South and Central America, it goes by the name *yuca* and is a favorite side dish with meat and fish.

Cassava root is also ground into flour, commonly known as *tapioca*. Its high starch content is utilized in puddings and custards. Tapioca is also made into pearls, common in Asian desserts and drinks, including *boba*, or bubble tea.

The juice of the cassava is combined with sugar and spices to create the sweet syrup called *cassareep* (see Appendix B), used in Asian and Caribbean cuisines.

Cassava can be found in Latin American markets, usually under the name yuca, both fresh and frozen. Tapioca flour and pearls are available at better supermarkets and Asian grocers. You can probably find cassareep in stores that carry Caribbean ingredients, or try online (wifglobal.com/Caribbeanpopularitems.htm).

Cassia

See Cinnamon.

Cayenne

See Appendix C.

Celery

A member of the botanical family *umbelliferae* (parsley)

Everyone is familiar with the stalks of this plant. Celery (*apium graveo-lens*) finds its way into everything. It's a vital member of French *mire-poix*, its crunchy texture enhances everything from turkey stuffing to tuna salad, and its afternoon snack appeal, slathered with peanut butter, is undeniable. But we often forget the appeal of the rest of the celery plant. The entire thing is edible—and delicious.

Celery's fresh, crisp flavor runs throughout the shiny jagged leaves, white flowers, and root. The variety known as celery root or celeriac (*apium graveolens rapaceum*) is delicious when peeled and boiled or shaved thin and eaten in salads.

The firm, dark seeds have a similar but stronger flavor. They're an important ingredient in all kinds of pickling, Worcestershire sauce, ketchup, barbecue sauce, coleslaw, and spice blends like Creole, Indian, and Bay.

Celery seeds, plants, and roots are commonly available at markets and nurseries.

Century Plant

See Agave.

Chameleon Plant

A member of the botanical family *saururaceae*

Also known as *fish mint* and *diep ca* (Vietnamese)

In the United States, the yellow, red, and green heart-shape leaves of this East Asian plant (*houttuynia cordata*) are valued largely for their beauty and heartiness as a perennial ground cover. But in Vietnam, both the leaves and rhizome find their way into the kitchen.

A typical ingredient in salads and spring rolls, chameleon plant leaves and roots have an aromatic taste of coriander and citrus.

Many Asian markets carry chameleon plant greens, and if you want to grow your own, they're even easier to find (naturehills.com).

Vietnamese Herb Salad

This salad is great eaten as is, but you can also wrap it in rice paper to make spring rolls. Or roll it into tortillas for a healthful wrap sandwich.

2 cups Napa cabbage, shredded
1 cup sorrel, chopped
1 cup chameleon plant leaves, chopped
1 cup perilla leaves, chopped
1 cup cilantro leaves
½ medium purple onion, sliced
1 cucumber, peeled, seeded, and sliced
1 clove garlic, minced
1 Thai chile, minced
1 tsp. honey
Zest and juice of 1 lime
1 TB. sesame oil
¼ cup fish sauce
¼ cup rice vinegar
Salt

1. In a large salad bowl, combine cabbage, sorrel, chameleon plant, perilla, cilantro, onion, and cucumber. Set aside.

2. In a jar with a tight-fitting lid, combine garlic, chile, honey, lime zest and juice, sesame oil, fish sauce, and vinegar. Close the lid and shake well. Season with salt and then pour dressing over salad greens with light hand.

 Hot Stuff

Be careful not to drown the greens in dressing when making this salad. Let the flavor of the herbs shine through. You'll be glad you did.

Chamomile

A member of the botanical family *asteraceae* (sunflower)

Also known as *mayweed*

You can find many varieties of this flowering plant, both annual and perennial, prized for both its ornamental beauty and its essential oil. But the most common culinary variety is German Chamomile (*matricaria recutita*). Like others of its species, chamomile has thin divided leaves and daisylike flowers with large cone-shape centers.

The flowers are dried and brewed into a tea that is well-known to soothe nerves. The flowers are rich in oil, and once dried, are used to flavor jams, jellies, puddings, cookies, and cakes. In addition, the Spanish use it to flavor their famous dry sherry *manzanilla*.

Dried chamomile is widely available in tea shops and health food stores.

Chervil

A member of the botanical family *umbelliferae* (parsley)

Also known as *French parsley*

Native to Eastern Europe and West Asia, chervil (*anthriscus cerefolium*) has long been a symbol of spring and is a part of many traditional Easter recipes as a symbol of renewal. In the past century, chervil has become an indispensable element of French cuisine. Its fine, lacy leaves and delicate white flowers have a slight anise flavor, which complements all sorts of foods, including fish, poultry, eggs, cheese, soups, and salads.

The beauty of this herb is all but lost when the herb is dried. It's best added fresh into recipes at the end of cooking, tossed into salads, or used as a fragrant garnish. Chopped fresh, it's a crucial ingredient in *fines herbes*, and the less-aromatic dried chervil is a component of *herbes de Provençe* (see Appendix B).

Chervil is available fresh at better supermarkets and at farmers' markets in the spring and summer. You can find or order seeds and seedlings at any nursery.

Chile Pepper

A member of the botanical family *solanaceae* (nightshade)

Known by many varietal names, such as *anaheim, cayenne, jalapeño,* and *poblano* (see Appendix C)

There are dozens of varieties of this New World native. Evidence of chile cultivation has been linked to several prehistoric tribes, from the tip of South America to the Great Plains of North America. They were known to the Aztecs, who are said to have harnessed the heat for ritualistic purposes. The Spanish brought the chile back to Europe, where it spread to the Far East. Today it's grown in all tropical regions.

All chile pepper varieties contain capsicum, a chemical compound that's perceived in the mouth as spicy heat. Capsicum heat has been measured extensively, and chiles are rated on the Scoville scale, named for Wilbur Scoville, who first rated capsicum's intensity in the early 1900s.

A pepper's heat is concentrated in the membrane found running through the center of the fruit from the interior stem. The seeds, which attach to the membrane, carry the heat, too, as does anything the membrane touches. Depending on your tolerance, you can cook chiles with or without the membrane and seeds. The flavor of the chile itself is often better appreciated without the intensity of the capsicum. Roasting, grilling, sautéing, and blanching all bring out different characteristics; dried and smoked, they take on still more personality. Dried and ground, their unique qualities are blended with other spices for specific cultural culinary applications (see Appendix B).

Hot Stuff

Capsicum is easily transferable through touch, so wear gloves and take care when cooking with chiles. One accidental touch to the eye is intensely painful, as is any contact with delicate dry or tender skin.

All varieties share similar characteristic shiny leaves and white flowers. The fruits range in size, and color varies from green through red, yellow, orange, and purple.

Chile peppers, either fresh or dried, are available at Latin American markets, many large supermarkets, and online (melissas.com). They're also very easy to grow, even for the novice gardener.

See also Appendix C.

Chili Powder

See Appendix B.

Hot Stuff

Chili or chile? When referring to the fruit, the word is spelled *chile*. When referring to the spicy stew, it's spelled *chili*. Chili powder is a spice blend made for use in the stew and, therefore, is spelled with an *i*. This can be confusing, because chili powder contains powdered chiles.

Chipotle

See Appendix C.

Chive

See Onion.

Cicely

A member of the botanical family *umbelliferae* (parsley)

Also known as *sweet cicely*, *anise fern*, and *great chervil*

The leaves of this perennial plant (*myrrhis odorata*) are like those of flat-leaf parsley or chervil, and like many in the parsley family, its flowers shoot up into flat tufts of tiny white blooms that give way to long, pointed seeds.

Cicely has a flavor similar to that of anise or licorice. The entire plant is edible, and most parts are used, although not extensively in the United States. Because of the plant's tolerance for low temperatures, it's better known in Scandinavia and Northern Europe.

The leaves are extremely sweet and are commonly combined with foods like rhubarb to reduce tartness. The seeds are very large and are added like cloves into spice mixes, cakes, and candies. They play a similar role to caraway and fennel seeds and can be found in herbal distilled spirits, including aquavit and chartreuse. The flowers are tossed into salads, and the root is boiled or sautéed and eaten as a vegetable. Tea made from the leaves is said to relieve upset stomach.

Fresh cicely is hard to find in American markets, although you might have some luck at a farmers' market in a real foodie town. You'll have better luck growing your own; look for seeds at garden centers (greenchronicle.com).

Cicely Strawberries and Cream

When sugar is tossed into fresh fruit, it pulls out the natural moisture, which creates a luscious sauce. Try it with all your fresh, ripe fruits.

2 pt. fresh, ripe strawberries, washed, trimmed, and halved
2 TB. sugar
½ cup cicely leaves, chopped
½ cup cicely blossoms
1 pt. heavy whipping cream
1 tsp. sugar
1 TB. cicely seeds, crushed

1. In a large bowl, combine strawberries, sugar, cicely leaves, and cicely blossoms. Toss to combine, cover, and set aside at room temperature for 1 or 2 hours.

2. Whip cream with sugar and cicely seeds until stiff peaks form. Set cream in the refrigerator until berries are ready.

3. To serve, spoon berries and their accumulated sweet juices in glass serving bowls and top with a dollop of whipped cicely cream. Serve with a crisp cookie.

Cilantro

See Coriander.

Cinnamon

A member of the botanical family *lauraceae* (laurel)

Both members of the laurel family, cinnamon (*cinnamomum verum*) and cassia (*cinnamomum aromaticum*) are combined into what we Americans recognize as cinnamon. The actual flavors are similar but are easily distinguishable when tasted side by side.

The spices come from the bark of Asian evergreen trees, harvested with much skill and tradition from trees 25 years or older. When the trees are still moist from seasonal rains, the inner bark is carefully stripped with special tools using techniques that have been passed down through many generations.

Cassia bark is much stronger than true cinnamon. In stick form, it's thicker and almost impossible to grind. True cinnamon bark is much finer and crumbles easily in the hand.

The buds and leaves are used in several Asian dishes and make delightful aromatic additions to candies, liqueurs, and potpourri. Cinnamon is a crucial element in many spice blends, including curries, barbecue rub, jerk rub, mulling spice, mole, and of course, pumpkin pie spice (see Appendix B).

Both cinnamon and cassia are readily available. Sticks sold whole in markets and specialty shops are usually clearly labeled as one or the other. If you happen across a bin of unmarked sticks in an ethnic market, remember that the hard ones are cassia and the brittle ones are cinnamon.

Cinnamon Basil

See Basil.

Citron

See Lemon.

Clove

A member of the botanical family *myrtaceae* (myrtle)

This incredibly tall evergreen tree (*syzygium aromaticum*) is native to the Molucca Islands (also known as the Spice Islands) in Southeast Asia. The name *clove* comes from the Latin *clavus*, which means "nail," and describes the shape and texture of the clove. The spice is a flower bud, picked when bright red, and dried. The result is a potent nugget of volatile oil, a natural anesthetic so strong it was commonly chewed to relieve toothaches. Cloves have long been appreciated for their aroma, burned as incense, smoked in cigarettes, and jabbed into citrus fruit as pomander balls.

Its popularity prompted a spice race of epic proportions, and domination of the Spice Islands jostled between the Portuguese, Spanish, British, and Dutch throughout the sixteenth and seventeenth centuries.

While the United States and much of Europe see the clove as a sweet spice, it's utilized in more savory applications in the East. Cloves easily find their way into curries, pickles, sausages, and spice mixes like *Chinese five-spice* (see Appendix B). It's an important element of classic French Béchamel sauce, where its character combines deliciously with onion and bay.

Cloves are available everywhere you find grocery carts.

Coffee

A member of the botanical family *rubiaceae* (bedstraw)

Also known by many species names, including *arabica* and *robusta*

This small tree (*coffea*), native to Ethiopia, is now grown all over the world, with major production in South and Central America. The tree bears a fruit called the coffee cherry, which, when ripe and red, are picked by hand. Each cherry holds two seeds, which are called beans. The beans are removed, dried, and exported. They are blended and roasted to bring out aromatic oils and then ground and brewed to produce, of course, the second most popular drink in the world (next to tea).

But besides the beverage, coffee is used to flavor many types of foods. Crushed or ground, these seeds can be steeped in any liquid to infuse their flavor. Try steeping beans in cream or milk for coffee custards, ices, and sauces. Grind beans to a fine powder to dust the outside of chocolate candies. Similarly, brewed coffee adds a pleasant bitterness to chocolate batters, not to mention pot roasts and barbecue sauces.

Coffee beans are widely available. Look for wide-eyed folks lingering with recycled paper cups and disposable income.

Beef Braised in Black Coffee

The deep, dark coffee flavor paired with acidic tomatoes and vinegar makes a mouthwatering combination that perfectly complements the moist, tender, slow-roasted beef.

2 or 3 lb. beef chuck roast or brisket
8 cloves garlic
4 slices bacon, diced
1 yellow onion, diced
2 stalks celery
1 (16-oz.) can crushed tomatoes
½ cup cider vinegar
4 cups strong black coffee
2 cups water
2 bay leaves
1 tsp. kosher salt
1 tsp. black pepper

1. Preheat the oven to 300°F.

2. Rinse beef and pat dry. On all sides of roast, make a total of 8 incisions with a boning knife, and insert 1 clove garlic into each one.

3. In a large roasting pan, cook bacon over high heat until brown and fat is rendered. Add onions and cook until translucent. Add roast, and brown on all sides. Add celery, tomatoes, vinegar, coffee, water, bay leaves, salt, and pepper. Bring liquid to a boil. At the boil, cover tightly with a lid or foil, and transfer to oven.

4. Roast for 6 to 8 hours or until fork tender. Slice meat thinly and serve with boiled potatoes or buttered noodles.

Coriander

A member of the botanical family *umbelliferae* (parsley)

Also known as *cilantro, Chinese parsley,* and *fresh coriander*

This annual herb (*coriandrum sativum*) was cultivated in ancient Egypt and has become an essential element in cuisines throughout Asia, India, South and Central America, Africa, and the Caribbean.

Coriander is grown for its seed as well as its leaves, known commonly as *cilantro*. The leaves are similar to and often mistaken for flat leaf parsley and chervil. To tell them apart, remember that the broad, divided leaves of cilantro are larger than chervil and have more rounded leaf tips than parsley. Of course, you can also tell them apart by taste.

Some people are put off by the flavor of cilantro at first, finding it bitter and soapy. But the unpleasant taste disappears when the herb is cooked. Fresh cilantro is used in conjunction with many spicy dishes, including chiles, salsas, curries, and soups, and it has a particular affinity for chile, garlic, and lime.

This herb's tiny pink flowers produce large pungent seeds that look like white peppercorns. Their flavor is that of strong citrus oil, and they're used whole or ground in many spice blends. They pop up in brines for vegetables and meats and are fundamental to curries and chili powders.

Cilantro and coriander are available in most large supermarkets and in Latin American markets.

Costmary

A member of the botanical family *asteraceae* (sunflower)

Also known as *Bible leaf, balsam herb*, and *alecost*

A native of Asia, costmary (*tanacetum balsamita*) is a lemony, minty, balsam-flavored leaf that was favored throughout medieval Europe and a common component of Elizabethan gardens. It was used as a bittering agent in brewing, before the common use of hops. Brought to America by colonists, costmary was steeped in wash water to discourage moths, and similarly used as a Bible bookmark, hence its name *Bible leaf.*

Its long, ovoid, jagged-edged light-green leaves add a fresh flavor to salads and stuffings and can be steamed or sautéed as a vegetable. When dried, it makes tea with a subtle bubblegum aroma.

It's not commonly available in markets, but it is a popular addition to herb gardens (richters.com).

Cream of Tartar

Tartaric acid

This is another mysterious white powder that, although not technically a spice or herb, can be found on nearly every spice shelf.

Crystals of tartaric acid accumulate on the interior walls of the barrels used to hold fermenting wine. The crystals are powdered and used in many culinary applications as an acidic ingredient. It loosens the protein of egg whites and aids in their whipping. It's added to liquefied sugar to prevent crystallization. In candy and frosting recipes, it promotes a creamy consistency. Before the advent of baking powder, cream of tartar was added to batters and dough as an acidic ingredient to activate baking soda. Occasionally, older recipes still call for that leavening combination.

Look for cream of tartar in the spice aisle.

Cress

A member of the botanical family *brassicaceae* (mustard)

There are *several edible species in the cress family, including watercress, garden cress, and winter cress.* Watercress (*nasturtium nasturtium-aquaticum*, although not related to the nasturtium flower), a fast-growing semi-aquatic perennial, is the most commonly eaten cress today. The thick, hollow stem; tiny, deep-green divided leaves; and small white flowers have a clean, peppery flavor.

Cress is native to Europe and Asia and is one of the oldest known leaf vegetables consumed by man. The Ancient Greeks believed it made them smarter, the Romans used it to cure baldness, and the Egyptians fed watercress juice to slaves to increase productivity. It grows prolifically in Southern England, and because it's highly nutritious, it has been a staple of the English diet for centuries. Full of vitamins, iron, and calcium—and low in cost—watercress has been eaten raw, mixed into salads, or sandwiched between bread by rich and poor alike. High in vitamin C, watercress was used to prevent scurvy long before citrus was available.

The ruffled, grassy leaves of garden cress (*lepidium sativum*) are easily distinguished from watercress, but they share a similar tangy pepper flavor. Garden cress is used in the same manner, in salads, sandwiches, and soups. It has pretty, edible orange flowers and small berries similar to capers, but it's also enjoyed early, as a sprout.

Winter cress (*barbarea vulgaris*), also known as *yellow rocket,* bears more resemblance to mustard in appearance, flavor, and use than other cress. Its wide leaves are valued as a sautéed vegetable as well as a salad green, and the seeds are pungent like mustard.

Watercress is available in better supermarkets and farmers' markets. Garden cress and winter cress are more difficult to buy fully grown. Try looking for them as baby plants and raising them as your own (kitchengardenseeds.com).

Cubeb Pepper

A member of the botanical family *piperaceae* (pepper)

Also known as *tailed pepper* and *Java pepper*

Originally grown in India, cubeb (*piper cubeba*) was popular in the Middle Ages, before black pepper was widely available. Brought to Europe by Arab traders, its use was eventually discouraged to advance the use of black pepper. Today the vine is grown in Java and Sumatra.

The long stalk produces berries that look like black peppercorns with a tail. Its spicy, gingery, pepper flavor is used extensively in Middle Eastern, Indonesian, and North African cuisines. It's also a common ingredient in gin and cigarettes.

Look for cubeb at Indian markets and on the Internet (www.silk.net/sirene).

Dates Stuffed with Cubeb and Parmesan

This is one of my all-time favorite food combinations. It sounds a little risky, but once you try it, you'll be hooked! It's a sure-fire hit for your next cocktail party.

1 cup freshly grated Parmesan cheese
1 tsp. ground cubeb pepper
1 pt. pitted medjool dates

1. Preheat the oven to 350°F.

2. In a small bowl, combine cheese and pepper and blend well.

3. Open each date, fill with cheese mixture, and pinch shut. Place filled dates on a cookie sheet, and bake for 10 minutes to warm through. Serve immediately.

Cuitlucoche

A member of the fungus species *ustilago maydis*

Also known as *huitlacoche, corn smut, maize mushroom,* and *Mexican truffle*

Technically, cuitlucoche isn't an herb or spice, but it is used in the same manner. Cuitlucoche is a fungus that grows on ears of corn. The Hopi, Zuni, and Aztec tribes have long considered it a delicacy, but farmers in the United States see it as a nuisance. Infected kernels expand as they fill with spores and become dark gray and black tumors or "galls." Don't let the appearance fool you, though. The smoky-sweet flavor, similar to mushrooms, is prized throughout Central America. It adds a delicious element to chile-cheesy recipes.

Fresh cuitlucoche is available fresh at some farmers' markets in the late summer. You can probably find it canned at most Latin American markets, although it's not as good as fresh.

Cuitlucoche and Corn Casserole

This recipe is put together like a classic *chilaquile* casserole, layered like lasagna with tortillas instead of noodles and chiles and cheese instead of tomato sauce. Look for *panella* cheese in Mexican markets, or substitute jack cheese.

4 TB. butter

1 large yellow onion, diced

4 cloves garlic, minced

2 roasted Anaheim, Poblano, or Pasilla chiles, diced

¼ cup fresh cilantro, chopped

¼ cup fresh epazote, chopped

1 lb. fresh or canned cuitlucoche

1 (10-oz.) pkg. frozen corn kernels

2 cups whipping cream

1 tsp. kosher salt

1 tsp. black pepper

8 to 10 corn tortillas

1 lb. panella cheese, grated

1. Preheat the oven to 350°F.

2. In a large sauté pan over high heat, melt butter. Add onion and sauté until golden brown. Add garlic, chiles, cilantro, and epazote, and continue cooking until tender. Add cuitlucoche, corn, and whipping cream, and stir. Reduce heat and simmer 5 minutes. Remove from heat.

3. In a casserole dish, layer cuitlucoche-corn mixture with tortillas and grated cheese, as you would lasagna, finishing with sauce and then cheese on the very top.

4. Cover casserole and bake for 30 minutes or until bubbly. Remove lid and bake 5 more minutes until the top is golden brown. Serve with fresh tomato salsa and sour cream.

Cumin

A member of the botanical family *umbelliferae* (parsley)

Also known as *Shah jeera*, *zeera*, and *geerah*

Like other members of the parsley family, the leaves of the cumin plant (*cuminum cyminum*) are thin and feathery, and the flowers are tiny white or pink. The distinctive striped or ridged seed grows in clusters after flowering. Its flavor is a little bitter and grassy but intensifies into a warm, musty flavor when toasted.

Native to the Mediterranean and the rivers of Egypt, cumin is mentioned in the Bible and was well-known in ancient Greece and Rome. In the Middle Ages, it was thought to promote fidelity and was consequently carried during wedding ceremonies.

The cumin seed is a favorite flavor worldwide, making a significant contribution to many cuisines. It is a base flavor in dishes and spice blends as diverse as Indian curries, Mexican moles, Arabic *baharat*, and American chili powder (see Appendix B).

Cumin is available whole and ground in most markets.

Curry

See Appendix B.

Curry Leaf

A member of the botanical family *rutaceae* (citrus)

From India and Sri Lanka, the small curry leaf tree (*murraya koenigii*) has matte green leaves that look like they could be from any citrus tree. But rubbed to a paste or steeped into liquids, they impart a unique, orangey, peanutlike fragrance that makes them a key ingredient in so much Indian and Sri Lankan cooking.

Prolonged cooking destroys the distinctive aroma, so curry leaves are best added at the end of a recipe. You'll see them floating like bay leaves in soups and broths, and they're often used to complement to fish, coconut, *dal*, *tandoor* cuisine, *nann*, and *paneer* cheese.

Curry leaf is available at Indian markets.

Dill

A member of the botanical family *umbelliferae* (parsley)

Also known as *dill seed* and *dill weed*

The fine, threadlike leaves of this delicate annual (*anthum graveolens*) have been used since the Middle Ages as an herbal remedy to relieve upset stomachs and gas and to protect against witchcraft.

Dill greens, flowers, and seeds are common accompaniments to cured fish, potatoes, and root vegetables. Dill is also used frequently in pickling, not just for cucumbers, but other vegetables as well. The aroma of all parts resembles caraway and anise but has a somewhat more sour, vinegary essence.

Dill, dill seed, and dried dill weed are readily available in most markets.

Dry Rub

See Appendix B.

Epazote

A member of the botanical family *chenopodiaceae*

Also known as *Mexican tea*, *skunk weed*, *pigweed*, and *wormseed*

Known mainly in Mexican cuisine, epazote (*chenopodium ambrosioides*) is a critical element in traditional bean dishes. When fresh, the jagged green leaves give off a potent kerosene aroma. But simmered long in stew and broths, they impart a subtle, peppery, bitter flavor very close to that of thyme. Most important, epazote is purported to alleviate the gaseous effects of the beloved bean.

Epazote is available in Latin American markets.

Epices Fine

See Spice Parisienne in Appendix B.

Fagara

See Szechwan Pepper.

Fennel

A member of the botanical family *umbelliferae* (parsley)

Also known as *finocchio* and *sweet anise* (the bulb)

Fennel (*foeniculum vulgare*) is native to the Mediterranean and thrives in similar climates. Bulb, leaves, stem, and seed all have a sweet anise scent and flavor. This prolific perennial can grow up to 6 feet tall. Its thin feathery leaves and flat, multi-flower heads are akin to dill. Of the several varieties, the Florence fennel (*foeniculum vulgare azoricum*) is grown mainly for its bulb, while the common fennel is used primarily for its seed, which is distinctively curved and ridged.

As a vegetable, fennel bulb is delicious grilled, sautéed, braised, or shaved thin and tossed raw into a salad. The seeds are best toasted and ground but turn up whole in tomato sauces, Italian sausages, and rye breads. They are believed to aid digestion, and consequently are an integral component of *mukhwas*, the colorful, sugar-coated seeds served after Indian meals to freshen breath and assist digestion.

Fennel stalks make excellent smoking matter, lit under roasting meats and fish to impart a unique flavor. Fennel pollen is a fine powder, easily airborne, coveted by adventurous chefs for its uncommon form and price tag as much as its flavor. It has the distinct scent of fennel with a hint of curry.

Fennel bulb and seeds are available in most markets.

Fenugreek

A member of the botanical family *fabaceae* (bean)

Also known as *methi, Greek hay,* and *goat's horn*

An annual in the bean family, fenugreek (*trigonella foenum-graecum*) grows like peas, with a thick stem, yellow sweet-pea–like flowers, and long, horn-shape seed pods that contain square yellow seeds. The seeds must be ground to release their maple-curry-nutty flavor.

Fenugreek is used in many spice blends, breads (Ethipoian *Injera*), confectionery (for its maple qualities), and pickling. The seed can also be ground into flour and used as a thickener.

Fenugreek sprouts and leaves have a similar, but sweeter, flavor than the seeds, are eaten as a vegetable, and mixed into dough, beans, and stews.

Blue Fenugreek (*trigonella caerulea*) is related, with a similar but subtler flavor and aroma, found in the alpine mountain regions of southeastern Europe. The leaves, seeds, flowers are used dried, and the herb is used extensively in alpine cheeses and breads of the region.

Find fenugreek in Middle Eastern, Indian, and African markets or on the Internet (penzys.com).

Filé

See Sassafras.

Fines Herbes

See Appendix B.

Finger Root

A member of the botanical family *zingiberaceae* (ginger)

Also known as *Chinese keys*

The finger root plant (*kaempferia pandurata*), native to Indonesia, is a tall, leafy biennial with beautiful pink tubular flowers shooting off from a long stalk. Its bright orange rhizome root is used throughout the cuisines of Southeast Asia. The flavor, while close to that of ginger, contains a hint of citrus and a bite of pepper.

Finger root is best used fresh and whole, as drying greatly diminishes its strength. Look for it in Asian markets.

Finger Root Ale

This homemade soda pop is a grown-up version of ginger ale. It has a small amount of alcohol, so serve it accordingly.

¼ cup freshly grated finger root
1 cup sugar
¼ tsp. active dry yeast
Zest and juice of 1 lime
Water

1. In a small bowl, combine finger root, sugar, yeast, lime zest and juice, and 2 cups water. Stir to combine.

2. Using a funnel, pour finger root mixture into a clean 2-liter plastic soda bottle. Fill the bottle with water to 2 inches below the cap. Seal the cap and place in a sunny window for 24 to 48 hours.

3. When the bottle feels very firm, chill it for 24 hours. Open chilled soda carefully, and serve, strained if desired.

 Hot Stuff

This ale has a small amount of alcohol. Also, soda left at room temperature for more than 48 hours, or in a location that is too hot, could explode.

Fish Boil

See Appendix B.

Fish Sauce

See Appendix B.

Five-Spice Powder, Chinese

See Appendix B.

Flax

A member of the botanical family *linaceae*

Also known as *linseed*

This tall annual plant (*linum usitatissimum*) has a thin stem, slender green leaves, and beautifully delicate pale blue flowers. Flax is grown for its oil-rich seed, as an ornamental plant, and for its stems, which when soaked and pounded provide fibers that are spun into cloth.

Flax oil was used for centuries to dry oil paint and varnish, but today it is prized for its omega-3 content. Essential fatty acids, the omega-3s have been found to reduce cholesterol, blood pressure, and plaque formation in arteries. Flax is a useful food source, especially for those with a diet low in fish, the most common source of omega-3. In addition, flax seeds are believed to reduce certain types of tumor growth and are taken as treatment of some forms of cancer.

The most common form of flax is oil, but more recently the seeds themselves have become a popular pantry addition. The nut-flavored seeds make a healthful addition to granolas, breads, and pilaf and are commonly ground as an egg replacement in vegan baking.

Flax and linseed oil are available at health food stores.

Vegan Oatmeal Cookies

This is a surprisingly good cookie, even for nonvegans.

1 TB. flax seeds
¼ cup plus 2 TB. water
½ cup vegetable oil
¼ cup soy milk
¾ cup brown sugar, packed
1 tsp. baking powder
½ tsp. cinnamon
1¾ cups rolled oats
1¼ cups all-purpose flour
1 cup raisins

1. Preheat the oven to 350°F. Line 2 baking sheets with parchment paper.

2. In a coffee grinder, grind flax seed to a fine powder.

3. In a large bowl, using a sturdy spoon, combine ground flax seed, water, oil, and soy milk, and stir well. Mix in brown sugar, baking powder, cinnamon, oats, flour, and raisins, and beat well to fully incorporate.

4. Drop cookies by the tablespoonful onto lined baking sheets 1 inch apart. Bake for 10 to 12 minutes or until golden brown on the edges. Cool cookies for 5 minutes before removing from the baking sheets.

Flower Pepper

See Szechwan Pepper.

Galangal

A member of the botanical family *zingiberaceae* (ginger)

Also known as *Laos root* and *China root*

This pale yellow-orange rhizome (*alpinia officinarum*) is striped with dark rings, and shoots out long, large leaves at the base of a thick stem topped with red and white flower buds.

Galangal was brought to Europe by Arab traders in the Middle Ages, but it fell out of favor when the more potent ginger hit the scene. Occasionally, old recipes pop up calling for galangal in mulled wines, cider, spiced meat, soups, and stews.

There are several varieties of galangal, all similar to ginger, but with a little zing of mustard heat and a floral or citrus essence. Native to Indonesia, galangal is favored in the cuisines of Vietnam (phõ soup), Thailand, and Malaysia.

Galangal is easy to find in Asian markets.

Old English Mulled Wine

This is a great recipe to warm you up on a cold winter day.

1 cup sugar
2 cups cream
2 cinnamon sticks, crushed
1 knuckle galangal, sliced
1 tsp. fresh grated nutmeg
1 tsp. black peppercorns, crushed
4 cardamom pods, crushed
1 bottle dry red wine, such as cabernet sauvignon

1. In a small saucepan, combine sugar, cream, cinnamon sticks, galangal, nutmeg, pepper, and cardamom. Bring to a simmer over medium heat, and gently warm for 15 minutes.

2. Turn off heat, add red wine, and steep another 15 minutes. Strain and serve warm.

Gale

A member of the botanical family *myricaceae* (myrtle)

Also known as *bog myrtle* and *sweet gale*

This evergreen shrub (*myrica gale*) grows profusely in the Scottish moors and bogs and was first used in medieval brewing before hops were readily available. The leaves and berries are very oily, and when boiled, wax rose to the surface and was gathered for use in candles.

As it's abundant in northern Europe, gale is occasionally mentioned as a flavoring in local soups and broths. The berries and leaves are steeped as a bay leaf would be and removed before serving. The flavor is similar to bayberry, with a slight eucalyptus-citrus aroma.

Gale is currently making a comeback as a favorite ingredient of home brewers, and as such is now available wherever home brewing supplies and ingredients are sold.

Garam Masala

See Appendix B.

Garlic

A member of the botanical family *liliaceae* (lily, onion)

Garlic (*allium sativum*) comes from Asia and is one of the oldest cultivated plants known to man. It is a perennial bulb (called a head) made up of divided cloves that are covered in papery skin. The strong sulfur scent of garlic has been known to repel insects (and vampires) and was thought to protect against disease and increase strength. Roman sailors and Egyptian slaves were given daily rations of garlic to ensure productivity.

Garlic is familiar in almost every cuisine worldwide. Its effect varies according to the way it's prepared. Juice squeezed from the cloves or cloves chopped fresh and raw add a pungent quality to recipes. Sautéed slowly or roasted whole, garlic's natural sugar is released and caramelized for a sweet buttery texture. Overcooked, and its bitterness is revealed.

There are several garlic varieties, and the flavor of one variety can vary by grower. The most common garlic in grocery stores is the soft-necked *allium sativum*. Purple striped *allium ophios* have a hard neck with a stem that's hard like a twig. Their flavor is rich, but the aroma is mild. Hard to find is the beautiful rose-colored garlic, with a dozen well-defined cloves visible around the outer edge, known as creoles. Elephant garlic is a different species, *allium ampeloprasm*, and has a softer taste.

Garlic is commonly available in supermarkets fresh, dried, ground, or mixed with salt. Use processed forms with care, as the flavor is concentrated and can easily overpower a dish.

Garum

See Appendix B.

Ginger

A member of the botanical family *zingiberaceae* (ginger)

Also known as *shoga*

This rhizome (*zingiber officinale*) heads up its own botanical family. Growing wild in Southeast Asia, ginger rhizomes produce a tall perennial plant with a broad stem, fat leaf blades that grow up the stalk, and tiny purple flowers.

The rhizome is used in several forms. It can be grated or sliced fresh, dried and ground to a powder, pickled in vinegar, or candied in sugar crystals or syrup. It plays a central role in all Asian cuisines, as both a central element and as part of more complex spice and herb combinations.

Once introduced to Europe, ginger became an indispensable element of medieval cookery. Its relevance in spiced foods has not diminished, and it's still used on its own or in conjunction with other sweet spices in baking.

Ginger can be found fresh in most supermarket produce sections and dried in the spice aisle.

Ginseng

A member of the botanical family *araliaceae*

Also known as *man root*

There are several varieties of ginseng, some native to America (*panax quinquefolius*), while others are native to Asia (*panax ginseng*). The low-growing plant produces vivid red flowers, but it's the root that's prized. Like ginger, ginseng root can be used fresh, dried, and steeped, or ground to a powder.

Ginseng's restorative powers have long been known around the globe. Native American tribes used wild ginseng as a love potion, to promote female fertility, and to treat respiratory ailments. Ancient Chinese medicine used ginseng to increase blood supply, improve circulation, and regain strength after illness. Today ginseng is thought to lower cholesterol, reduce stress, and enhance strength.

Although most commonly seen in tea form, ginseng is also used to flavor soups and broths, gum and candy, toothpaste, cigarettes, and America's favorite lemon-lime soda pop, 7-Up.

Ginseng is available in Asian markets.

Korean Chicken Soup

Samgyetang is the Korean name for this soup, which is used not only as a cure, but as a sickness preventive as well. You might find many variations, including those with sticky rice and dried jujube fruit.

2 qt. chicken broth
4 cloves garlic, minced
¼ cup grated ginseng
1 cup rice
¼ cup fresh pitted dates, chopped
2 TB. soy sauce
1 TB. chile paste
2 cups cooked chicken, shredded
1 cup green onions, chopped
2 TB. toasted sesame seeds

1. In a large soup pot, combine broth, garlic, and ginseng, and bring to a boil. Add rice, reduce heat, and simmer, covered, for 20 minutes.

2. Add dates, soy sauce, chile paste, and chicken, and simmer another 20 minutes. Serve hot, garnished with green onions and sesame seeds.

Goma

See Sesame.

Golpar

A member of the botanical family *umbelliferae* (parsley)

Also known as *hogweed*

A giant member of the parsley family, golpar (*heracleum mantegaz-zianum*) produces seeds common to Iranian cuisine. Ground or used whole in breads and pastries, the flavor is close to that of a mustardy celery seed. You'll also find golpar accompanying fruits, and its anti-gas effects make it an obvious ingredient in slow cooked bean recipes. You can also enjoy leaves and leaf stems pickled.

The plant itself is banned in the United States, as it produces a noxious sap that's quite painful on the skin and can cause a lot of damage, especially if ingested.

You can find the seeds in Arabic markets and online.

Pomegranate Salad

Native to Iran and the Himalayas, pomegranates also thrive in the drier climates of California and Arizona. The juice—high is vitamin C, folic acid, and antioxidants—is a popular drink worldwide and is thickened and sweetened to make Grenadine syrup.

2 cups pomegranate seeds
3 mandarin oranges, sectioned and cut into small pieces
1 cup walnuts, toasted and chopped
½ tsp. golpar
½ tsp. sea salt

1. Combine pomegranate seeds, oranges, walnuts, golpar, and salt, and toss well to combine.

2. Marinate at room temperature for 1 or 2 hours before serving.

Green Onion

See Onion.

Green Peppercorn

See Pepper.

Gremolata

See Appendix B.

Grains of Paradise

> A member of the botanical family *zingiberaceae* (ginger)
>
> Also known as *Guinea pepper, ginger pepper, alligator pepper,* and *meleguenta pepper*

Grains of paradise come from a perennial reedlike plant of West Africa (*aframomum melegueta*). From swampy terrain sprout narrow bamboo-like leaves with pink-purple flowers growing at the base. The flowers are trumpet shaped, like lilies, and produce long seed pods. Each pod contains many seeds whose flavor is a cross between pepper, ginger, coriander, and cardamom.

Grains of paradise were used throughout the Middle Ages before pepper became readily available. Many medieval spice powders include grains of paradise as their base. The name was an advertisement of sorts, enticing men to come in search of the spice along the West African pepper coast. But as trade for black pepper became easier, grains of paradise fell out of favor.

Today the spice is well-known throughout Morocco and Tunisia and is used in specialty brewing, distillation, and more adventurous confectionery.

Buy grains of paradise on the Internet (thespicehouse.com) and in Middle Eastern markets.

Lemon Cake with Grains of Paradise and Rosemary

This cake is best served the day it is made. Top it with a dollop of crème fraiche (a tangy thickened cream) or lightly sweetened whipped cream. If you have any leftovers, try eating it toasted, spread with cream cheese.

2¼ cups cake flour
1 tsp. baking powder
¼ tsp. salt
2 sticks butter
1 cup sugar
Zest of 4 lemons
1 TB. grains of paradise, ground
4 eggs
2 TB. milk
1 cup confectioners' sugar, sifted
1 tsp. fresh rosemary, chopped very fine
¼ cup lemon juice

1. Preheat the oven to 325°F. Line a 9x6-inch loaf pan with butter and parchment paper.

2. In a large bowl, sift together flour, baking powder, and salt, and set aside.

3. In another large bowl, and with a sturdy spoon or electric mixer, cream together butter, sugar, lemon zest, and grains of paradise until light and fluffy. Add eggs, one by one. Add milk, and slowly add sifted ingredients.

4. Pour batter into the loaf pan and bake for 45 to 60 minutes or until a pick inserted at the center of cake comes out clean. Cool cake for 10 minutes before inverting onto a rack.

5. Make glaze by mixing confectioners' sugar, rosemary, and lemon juice. Drizzle over warm cake. Cool before slicing.

Guajillo

See Appendix C.

Gum Arabic

A member of the botanical family *fabaceae* (bean)

Here's another example of a common ingredient that's not a spice but nevertheless finds its way onto spice shelves. Extracted from the bark of a deciduous acacia tree (*acacia senegal*) of sub-Saharan Africa, gum arabic is used to thicken and emulsify foods. In confectionery, gum arabic is useful in preventing crystallization, especially in recipes with low moisture and high sugar, like gummy bears and marshmallows. It's also used in brewing and soft drinks, causing the fizzy foams to stick to the side of a glass.

Buy gum arabic in shops specializing in pastry and candy-making supplies.

Habanero

See Appendix C.

Harissa Sauce

See Appendix B.

Herbes de Provençe

See Appendix B.

Hijiki

From the family *sargassaceae* (brown algae)

(Algae are technically neither plant nor animal.)

Found along the rocky shoreline of Japan, this algae (*hizikia fusiformes*) is a traditional element of the Japanese diet. Rich in fiber and minerals, hijiki is dried and packaged in thin strips and then prepared by either soaking or simmering. Its slightly sweet flavor is used to enhance soups, vegetables, fish, and rice.

Look for hijiki in Japanese markets.

Hoisin

See Appendix B.

Hop

From the botanical family *cannabidaceae*

The rhizome of this perennial (*humulus lupulus*) shoots off vines up to 25 feet long every year. Its flowers develop into cones that consist of layers of papery, tannic petals concealing powdery yellow aromatic resin used extensively in brewing for both its flavor and its preservative qualities. Hop has been grown in Germany since the eighth century for use as a dye and a natural sedative, and Germany is still an important producer. Hop vines can be seen throughout the German countryside climbing up poles throughout the summer.

Dried hop cones are used in brewing, and young shoots of hops are considered a delicacy, and served steamed or sautéed with vinaigrette or deep-fried like tempura.

Dried hops are available wherever home brewing supplies and ingredients are sold. Look for fresh hops online (www.essentiallyhops. co.uk).

Horehound

A member of the botanical family *labiatae* (mint)

Horehound is a dark-green perennial (*marrubium vulgare*) with clover-like white flowers that grow up the stem. The stems and leaves, which are covered in white fuzz, are steeped as a cough remedy. Turned into drops and candy for similar purpose, the grown-up flavor became popular at the turn of the twentieth century.

Horehound is available dried online (glenbrookfarm.com) or as seed (richfarmgarden.com).

Horehound Candy

My Grandpa Reed introduced this candy to me when I was a kid. He bought me some at the old-time candy shop in Roaring Camp, an old-time railroad in the Santa Cruz Mountains. The flavor still makes me think of trains.

2 cups water
½ cup horehound leaves, chopped
2 cups brown sugar
2 cups granulated sugar
½ tsp. lemon juice

1. In a small saucepan, combine water and horehound leaves. Bring to a boil, remove from heat, and steep for 1 hour. Strain out leaves.

2. In a small saucepan, combine strained horehound water, brown sugar, and granulated sugar, and bring to a boil over high heat. At the boil, add lemon juice and insert a candy thermometer. Cook until syrup reaches 300°F, or hard crack stage.

3. Spoon syrup on buttered waxed paper in nickel-size lozenges. When cool, dust with granulated sugar. Wrap pieces individually in parchment paper, waxed paper, or candy wrappers. Store in an airtight container.

Horseradish

A member of the botanical family *cruciferae* (mustard, cabbage)

Also known as *horse root* and *mountain radish*

Native to Eastern Europe, this perennial (*armoracia rusticana*) is identified by its huge leaves and loose white flowers that grow at the top of a tall stalk, not unlike mustard. The leaves, one of the Passover Seder bitter herbs, are quite tasty when cooked like spinach, steamed or sautéed with garlic and butter. But it's the root that gets most of the attention.

Peeling through the horseradish's dirty brown outer skin reveals the tender white root, full of oils similar to those found in its cousin, the mustard seed. It's spicy hot, especially near the skin, and is grated and incorporated into dressings and sauces to be served alongside meat, sausage, and fish. Once grated, the oils dissipate rapidly.

Horseradish is available fresh or prepared in most supermarkets.

Roasted Horseradish Beets

Beets are delicious, but they do make a mess. Many cooks wear gloves when peeling and slicing them to spare their hands from the magenta dye.

6 large beets
2 large yellow onions
1 head garlic
½ cup freshly grated horseradish
12 TB. cider vinegar
2 TB. brown sugar
2 cups sour cream
1 tsp. kosher salt

1. Preheat the oven to 450°F.

2. Wrap whole beets together in a large piece of aluminum foil. Wrap whole onions together in another large piece of aluminum foil. Wrap garlic head in another small piece of aluminum foil. Place all the foil packets on a baking sheet, and roast until tender, about 30 minutes for garlic and about 1 hour for onions and beets. Cool completely.

3. Cut roasted garlic bulb in half and squirt out soft garlic paste. Combine garlic paste in a large bowl with horseradish, vinegar, brown sugar, sour cream, and salt. Mix well to combine.

4. Unwrap beets and carefully peel off skin. (Watch out! It stains.) Slice peeled roasted beets into wedges. Peel roasted onions and cut in the same manner as beets.

5. Add beets and onions to the bowl and toss to thoroughly combine. Serve hot, warm, or cold.

Hyssop

A member of the botanical family *labiatae* (mint)

A shrubby plant with narrow leaves, hyssop (*hyssopus officinalis*) is often confused with tarragon. The flavor, however, is less like the anise hint of tarragon and more like a combination of thyme and rosemary.

Hyssop is best used fresh, and the entire plant is edible, including the tiny purple flowers, which are lovely tossed into salads and vegetable dishes. Like thyme and rosemary, hyssop melds well with many flavors as diverse as heavy meats, legumes, and even fruits. Hyssop is one of the many herbs infused into the French distilled *Chartreuse*.

Hyssop tea is available in health food stores, or you can grow your own plants from seeds (greenchronicle.com).

Jalapeño

See Appendix C.

Jerk

See Appendix B.

Juniper

A member of the botanical family *cupressaceae* (cypress)

A shrubby, spiny-needled evergreen native to southern Europe, juniper (*juniperus communis*) is prized for its deep purple berries full of aromatic oils that may be most recognized as the main flavor component of gin.

Crushed or whole, dried juniper berries are a common ingredient to pickling brines, marinades, sauerkraut, and mustards. They are a traditional seasoning of lamb and heavy game meat and poultry. Their heavy, woody flavor cuts through fatty, pungent flavors. Juniper berries, however, are quite pungent, so use them with a light hand. A little goes a long way.

Juniper berries are available in better supermarkets.

Martini Bread

Serve this with softened butter and a gin martini, shaken not stirred.

2 TB. active dry yeast
1 cup warm water
2 TB. sugar
4 TB. butter, softened
1 tsp. salt
2 tsp. juniper berries, ground
½ cup pimiento-stuffed Spanish olives, chopped
2 or 3 cups bread flour

1. In a large bowl, combine yeast and water, and stir to combine. Add sugar, butter, salt, juniper berries, and olives, and mix well. Add flour, 1 cup at a time, until a firm dough forms.

2. Turn out dough onto a table, and knead for 8 to 10 minutes until dough is smooth and elastic. Add more flour, a little at a time, as needed. Cover dough with a warm damp towel and let rise until doubled in volume, 1 or 2 hours.

3. Preheat the oven to 375°F.

4. Form dough into a smooth, long loaf shape and place on a baking sheet lined with parchment paper. Sprinkle dough lightly with flour, and bake until golden brown and firm, about 30 minutes. Cool completely before slicing.

Kaffir Lime

A member of the botanical family, *rutaceae* (citrus)

The kaffir lime tree (*citrus hystrix*) produces a fruit, but its zest and juice are nowhere near as potent or popular as its unique double lobed, figure-8 leaf. The leaf's intense aroma is an essential ingredient throughout Southeast Asia. You'll find it floating in broths, soups (*pho, tom kha gai*), and curries and combined with other herbs and spices like garlic, galangal, and chiles.

The fruit is bright green and very bumpy and is no substitute for the intense lime aroma of the leaves.

Kaffir lime leaves are available at Asian markets.

K

Thai Chicken Soup with Coconut

In Thailand the name of this soup is *Thom Kha Gai*. The flavor combination of kaffir leaves, coconut, lemongrass, and galangal is heavenly.

1 (5.6-oz.) can coconut milk
4 cups chicken broth
¼ cup fresh galangal, grated
2 stalks lemongrass, cut into 2-in. pieces
4 TB. fish sauce (nam pla)
6 kaffir lime leaves, crushed
2 Thai chiles, minced
3 cups cooked chicken, shredded
2 limes, cut into wedges
¼ cup fresh cilantro, chopped

1. In a large soup pot, combine coconut milk, chicken broth, galangal, and lemongrass. Bring to a boil, reduce heat, and simmer for 30 minutes. Strain and return liquid to the pot.

2. Add fish sauce, kaffir lime leaves, Thai chiles, and chicken. Simmer for 30 minutes more. Serve hot with lime wedges and chopped cilantro.

Kecap Manis

See Appendix B.

Kenchur

A member of the botanical family *zingiberaceae* (ginger)

Used in Asian curries and stir-fries, the kenchur rhizome (*kaempferia galangal*) looks like dark baby ginger. The flavor, however, is less like ginger and more like a cross between cardamom and eucalyptus. It is used in spice blends and spicy pastes to flavor vegetables, noodles, rice, and tofu.

Find Kenchur in powdered form in Asian markets.

Kinome

See Szechwan Pepper.

Kochu Chang

See Appendix B.

Kombu

From the family *laminariaceae* (kelp)

(Kelp is technically neither a plant nor an animal.)

Also known as *konbu*

This dark brown sea vegetable (*laminaria japonica*) is widely eaten in Northeast Asia. Sun-dried, it's used to flavor sushi, vegetables, and soups and is an essential ingredient in the Japanese broth *dashi*. Cooked with beans, it's thought to relieve their gaseous effect. Kombu is available whole, shredded, powdered, and pickled.

Also from kombu come glutamic acid, an ingredient in *MSG* (monosodium glutamate), and the basis of the taste *umami*.

Kombu is available in Japanese markets.

Kosher Salt

See Salt.

Ku Chai

See Onion.

Laurel

See Bay.

Lavender

A member of the botanical family *lamiaceae* (mint)

This common perennial shrub grows in any Mediterraneanlike climate. The stem becomes very woody over the years, shooting off stiff, thin stalks. The leaves are silvery gray and bushy at the base of the stem, and at the top sits the skinny purple flowers, loaded with aromatic oil.

An ancient cure for headaches, lavender's restorative powers are still extolled by aroma therapists. The flavor is floral, although some consider it soapy. In fact, lavender has been used in wash water since ancient times. The name comes from the Latin *lavare*, meaning "to wash," and is the root of the word *lavatory* (wash room) and the Spanish *lavanderia* (laundry).

There are many varieties of lavender, including common (*lavandula officinalis*), English (*lavandula angustifolia*), French (*lavandula dentate*), and Spanish (*lavandula stoechas*).

Lavender is an integral part of the French seasoning blend *herbes de Provençe* (see Appendix B), but on its own it enhances all kinds of foods, just like its cousins rosemary, oregano, and sage. On the sweet side of the kitchen, lavender has become popular as a dessert flavor, used in combination with fruits, chocolate, and vanilla.

Look for lavender in Latin American markets, health food stores, and specialty grocers.

Purple Potatoes with Lavender

If you've never seen a purple potato, don't be afraid! They're dark gray skin conceals a beautifully vibrant purple flesh that tastes like a sweeter version of any average potato.

8 to 10 small purple Peruvian potatoes
Water
1 tsp. kosher salt
6 TB. unsalted butter
¼ cup lavender buds, crushed
1 tsp. sea salt

1. In a large saucepan, cover potatoes with water, add kosher salt, and boil until potatoes are tender. Strain water off potatoes and set aside to cool. When cool, slice potatoes into medallions.

2. In a large sauté pan, melt butter over medium heat. Add lavender and cook until butter solids turn dark brown. (Don't be alarmed if they turn a little black—that just adds to the flavor.) Add potatoes and sea salt, and toss to coat. Serve immediately.

Leek

See Onion.

Lemon

A member of the botanical family *rustaceae* (citrus)

There are about 50 varieties of lemon (*citrus limonum*), but all are derived from the Citron, a large bumpy lemon with a very thick rind and comparatively little fruit inside. The citron was first used in India, spreading to Persia, Babylonia, and finally Europe with the help of Alexander the Great. The Buddha's hand (*citrus sarcodactyla*), a Chinese variety, is unusual looking, with fingerlike lobes. Other more common varieties include the Meyer, Eureka, Lisbon, Fino, and Verna. Trees can reach 12 feet high, and most have straggly branches covered with thorns, shiny evergreen leaves, and fragrant white flowers that produce the fruit each winter.

Lemons are cultivated throughout the Mediterranean, Greece, Spain, Italy, and North Africa, but more are grown in California than in all of Europe combined.

Lemon oil, pressed from skins that remain after juicing, is becoming a popular ingredient. Lemon oil and lemon extract are available in better supermarkets.

Lemon Balm

A member of the botanical family *lamiaceae* (mint)

The fat, pointy leaves of this lush perennial (*melissa officinalis*) have a lemony, minty flavor that's a common addition to tea, mulled wine, ice cream, fruit compotes, and candies.

As a tea, lemon balm was traditionally used as a stress reliever and fever reducer. It's a favorite of bees (*melissa* is Greek for "bee") and was commonly planted around orchards to attract them for pollination.

Fresh lemon balm is occasionally available at farmers' markets. You can grow your own from seeds (greenchronicle.com) or look for it dried (mountainroseherbs.com).

Lemon Balm Sherbet

A sherbet is a frozen fruit dessert made with milk. If you replace the milk with water, juice, or fruit purée, it becomes a sorbet.

2 cups granulated sugar
2 cups water
2 cups lemon balm leaves, chopped
¼ tsp. kosher salt
2 qt. whole or nonfat milk

1. In a medium saucepan, combine sugar, water, and lemon balm leaves, and bring to a boil over high heat. At the boil, remove from heat and cool completely.

2. Strain leaves out of cooled syrup, and combine syrup with salt and milk. Process in an ice-cream machine following the manufacturer's instructions. Serve with fresh berries and crisp cookies.

Lemon Basil

See Basil.

Lemon Myrtle

A member of the botanical family *myrtaceae* (myrtle)

Also known as *sweet verbena*

This bushy tree (*backhousia citriodora*) from the rainforests of Queensland is a major producer of *citral*, the oil responsible for all things lemony. Leaves of the lemon myrtle contain as much as 95 percent citral. To put that in perspective, lemongrass contains 65 percent, and lemons have a mere 5 percent.

So what do you do with a flavor more lemony than a lemon? Seafood and poultry recipes come to mind first, but it's a good choice for dairy recipes that would ordinarily be curdled by the acid of lemon juice. Ice cream, custards, and cream sauces can all be steeped with the leaf of the lemon myrtle to impart the lemony goodness.

Ask your Australian friends to send you some lemon myrtle, or look for it on the Internet (www.thespiceshop.co.uk).

Lemon Verbena

A member of the botanical family *verbenaceae* (verbena)

Also known as *bee brush*

Native to South and Central America, lemon verbena (*aloysia triphylla*) is a perennial, deciduous shrub with long thin leaves and clusters of tiny purple flowers. The shrubs, sometimes growing upward of 30 feet, were brought to Europe by Spanish explorers, where it has thrived.

The leaves are sticky with oil that produces a sweet, lemony scent that's much loved in soaps, perfumes, jams, and jellies. It's a natural addition to simmering seafood and poultry and rice dishes, and makes great tea, fruits sorbets, and cocktails.

Verbena is available dried in tea shops and health food stores and occasionally shows up fresh at farmers' markets.

Lemongrass

A member of the botanical family *poaceae* (sugarcane, bamboo)

Also known as *citronella* and *sereh*

Originally from Asia, lemongrass (*cymbopogon citrates*) is easily grown in any mild climate. The grassy stalk is woody and fibrous, but when pounded and infused into liquid, it imparts an exotic lemon essence. Like *lemon myrtle* and *lemon verbena*, it's the essential oil *citral* that is responsible for lemongrass's flavor. The best-quality lemongrass should be fresh and still green.

Lemongrass is a major ingredient in Thai and Vietnamese cuisine, but it can be used wherever lemony flavor is welcome. Look for it in Asian markets.

Licorice

A member of the botanical family *fabaceae* (legume)

The bushy licorice plant (*glycyrrhiza glabra*) grows about 3 feet high and has delicate thin leaves, furry seedpods, and creamy pink pealike flowers. But it's the root that is prized above all. It was known by the ancient Greeks, and bits of licorice root are said to have been found in King Tut's tomb.

Naturally sweeter than table sugar, licorice root has long been chewed as a breath freshener, or sliced and added to teas, liqueurs, stews, and soups. When the roots are pounded and the juice extracted, it can be solidified into black sticks or drops. This pure licorice is eaten as candy and as a natural cough drop and expectorant. It's added as a sweetener for liqueurs and teas, too.

Most licorice candy today is highly sweetened and flavored with anise, but in some parts of Europe and Scandinavia, licorice candy is made the old-fashioned way, with lots of salt.

Although difficult to grind, licorice sticks can be steeped into stews, used as skewers for kebabs, or as smoking wood for barbecues. Licorice extract is available at stores specializing in confectionery supplies, but dried root will take a trip on the Internet (kalyx.com).

Lily Bud

A member of the botanical family *hermerocallidaceae*

Also known as *golden needles*, *tiger lily buds*, and *pinyin*

The dried, unopened buds of orange and yellow day lilies, (*hemerocallis fulva*) are an ancient ingredient in Chinese cooking. Their musky, earthy flavor is common in stir-fries, hot and sour soup, and moo shu pork.

Look for buds that are pale in color and flexible, not dry and brittle. Be sure to soak lily buds in warm water before adding them to recipes.

Lily buds are readily available in Asian markets.

Stir-Fried Pork with Lily Buds

This stir-fry tastes just as good with beef, chicken, or shrimp.

½ cup lily buds
2 cups hot water
1 TB. peanut oil
2 cloves garlic
1 tsp. fresh ginger, grated
¼ cup cilantro, chopped fine
1 stalk celery, chopped thinly
1 lb. pork tenderloin, sliced thin
2 tsp. fish sauce
1 tsp. honey
½ cup chopped cashews
1 TB. sesame seeds

1. Soak lily buds in hot water for 20 minutes, until soft. Slice in half and discard tough ends. Set aside.

2. Heat a wok over high heat and add peanut oil. Add garlic, ginger, cilantro, and celery, and fry, stirring, until translucent. Add pork and fry, stirring, until cooked through. Add lily buds, fish sauce, and honey, and stir until warmed through.

3. Serve over steamed rice sprinkled with cashews and sesame seeds.

Lime

A member of the botanical family *rutaceae* (citrus)

The common lime tree (*citrus acida*) is smaller than other citrus, grow-ing only about 10 feet tall. Like many of its citrus cousins, the lime tree has prickly branches and small, fragrant white flowers.

Introduced from Persia to Europe during the crusades, lime became highly prized for its oil-rich zest and floral aroma. Because the lime is high in vitamin C, British sailors ate a daily ration of lime to prevent scurvy (that's where the nickname *Limey* originated).

Lime juice is used throughout Central and South America as an acidic ingredient to flavor foods and to cook seafood *ceviche*. Dried limes are common in Persian cuisine, and the *kaffir lime* leaf is com-mon throughout Southeast Asia. The most common varieties include the Persian lime (*citrus latifolia*), which grows without thorns or seeds, and the Key or Mexican lime (*citrus aurantifolia*), which is much smaller and more fragrant. Both turn yellow when ripe but are usually picked green.

Most grocers stock the Persian lime, but depending on where you live you may have to go to a Latin American market or specialty grocer to find Key or Mexican limes.

Lovage

A member of the botanical family *umbelliferae* (parsley)

Also known as *alexanders*

Common throughout southern Europe, this hearty perennial (*levisticum officinale*) has a thick hollow stem that can grow quite tall. Its shiny tri-leaflets look a lot like celery leaves, and it has large flat pom-poms of small yellow flowers.

Its celerylike appearance is a clue to its flavor. The seeds are often mistaken (or substituted) for celery seed. Fresh or dried, the leaves, seeds, and stems are used in salads, breads, added to potatoes, eggs, meat, and fish. The root, too, can be boiled and eaten like celery root.

Lovage is occasionally found at fancier farmers' markets, but your best bet is to grow your own (greenchronicle.com).

Lovage-Poached Shrimp Salad

Used in poaching liquid, lovage lends it essence to the shrimp without overpowering. It's a great way to feature flavors subtly.

2 cups white wine
1 ½ cup lovage, chopped
Juice of 1 lemon
1 TB. black peppercorns, crushed
1 lb. medium shrimp, peeled and deveined
1 tsp. Dijon mustard
1 cup olive oil
1 tsp. sea salt
½ tsp. black peppercorns, ground
2 stalks celery, chopped fine
2 green onions, chopped fine
1 avocado, diced
4 cups mixed baby green lettuces, washed and dried

1. In a large pot, combine wine, 1 cup lovage, juice of ½ lemon, and crushed peppercorns. Bring to a boil and simmer 30 minutes. Remove from heat, strain liquid, and add raw shrimp. Return to heat and simmer until shrimp are pink, about 5 minutes. (Do not overcook.) Drain shrimp and cool.

2. In a large bowl, mix together mustard, remaining ½ cup lovage, remaining lemon juice, olive oil, sea salt, and ground black pepper. Add celery, onions, shrimp, avocado, and baby greens, and toss to combine.

Mace

See Nutmeg.

Maché

A member of the botanical family *valerianaceae* (valerian)

Also known as *corn salad*, *lambs lettuce*, and *field lettuce*

Native to the Mediterranean, the tangy, nutty flavor of this delicate salad green (*valerianella locusta*) is a well-kept secret. The dark green leaves have a soft velvety texture that blends well with stronger salad greens. Used mostly fresh, it can also be added successfully to eggs and other vegetable dishes.

Maché is available from specialty growers and at farmers' markets. You can also grow your own (horizonherbs.com).

Mahleb

A member of the botanical family *rosaceae* (rose)

This spice is made from the pits of a very tart black cherry (*prumus mahaleb*) that's ground into flour. The flavor is a bit fruity, with some characteristics of marzipan—which makes sense, as cherries are cousins to the almond.

Hailing from the eastern Mediterranean, mahleb is well-known in the cuisines of Greece, Lebanon, and Armenia. Ground into flour, the pits are used to thicken meat and vegetable stew and lentils, and are incorporated into breads.

Mahleb is available in Arabic markets.

Mahleb Date Bars

Dates are an ancient sweet treat. Before sugar, dates and other dried fruits were the candy of the "common folk."

1 egg
1 cup sugar
½ tsp. salt
1 TB. mahleb, finely ground
1 tsp. anise seed, finely ground
½ cup milk
2 tsp. baking powder
1 cup all-purpose flour
1½ cup dates, pitted and chopped
1 cup walnuts, chopped
2 cups confectioners' sugar, sifted

1. Preheat the oven to 350°F. Lightly butter a 9×13-inch cake pan.

2. In a large bowl, stir together egg and sugar. Add salt, mahleb, anise, and milk, and stir to combine.

3. In a separate bowl, sift together baking powder and flour. Fold in dates and walnuts.

4. Pour batter into the prepared pan, and bake for 20 to 30 minutes or until golden brown. Cool completely, cut into bars, and roll each bar in confectioners' sugar. Store in an airtight container at room temperature for 1 week, or freeze for up to 1 month.

M

Mango Powder

See Amchoor.

Marigold

A member of the botanical family *asteraceae* (sunflower)

These round orange and yellow flowers (*calendula officinalis*) are common in the home garden as an ornamental, but the petals have long been used in the kitchen. Their spicy flavor was common throughout the Middle Ages, added to wines, grains, cakes, and puddings.

Today, marigolds are a popular edible flower, tossed into salads and cold soups. As a colorant, marigolds are often used as a substitute for saffron, and they are commonly fed to chickens to color egg yolks and skin.

You can get marigold plants and seeds at any nursery.

Marjoram

A member of the botanical family *labiatae* (mint)

Also known as *sweet marjoram, French marjoram,* and *wild marjoram*

Marjoram is in the same family and species as oregano (*origanum*), and the flavors are very similar. In fact, they may be difficult to distinguish at first glance. But taste them side by side, and you'll find that marjoram is more delicate and the flavor more subtle. Marjoram combines a peppery hint of many related herbs, like rosemary and lavender, with no one flavor overwhelming. Perhaps this is why marjoram is a part of so many herb blends. Its long, thin, twiggy stem is sparsely dotted with tiny round green leaves and white or pink flowers.

Marjoram is a natural with many savory foods, including soups, vegetables, meat, and fish. But it can be surprisingly good with sweeter foods, too. Try steeping it with lemonade for a refreshing summer drink, or mixing it with fruit.

Look for fresh marjoram at better grocers and farmers' markets. Dried marjoram is readily available at most supermarkets.

Masala

See Appendix B.

Chefspeak

Masala is a term that describes a mixture of spices. You can find dozens of variations from every region in India.

Mint

A member of the botanical family *labiatae* (mint)

Several species, including *spearmint* and *peppermint*

M

Members of the *menthe* species all share similar characteristics. They are perennial, coming back year after year stronger than ever. If you've ever had mint growing in your yard, you know what I mean. It's spread by seed and creeping rhizomes, and it takes charge of the garden. All of the menthes have four-sided stems, paired leaves, and small cloverlike flowers. Mint leaves can be cut and dried or used fresh.

Spearmint is the most common mint used in the kitchen. Its flavor is most associated with gum or toothpaste and the leaf is used most often to dress up dessert plates. Recognize it by its thick, wrinkled leaves and clearly defined veins. Peppermint has the flavor of a candy cane and is the mint most often used in extract form. Its leaves are darker, shinier, and smoother than spearmint. Black peppermint is very dark green with purple stems, and its oil is quite strong. White peppermint has a green stem, and its flavor is more subtle.

Mint oil contains *menthol*, which induces a familiar sensation that numbs the mouth. It's a natural antiseptic and anesthetic and has been used for centuries in liqueurs, soaps, and teas. It settles an upset stomach, aids digestion, is used as a diuretic, and also serves as an insecticide.

In the West, we associate mint with sweeter foods, but it has savory application in the East. Beans, grains, and meats all get the mint treatment in the Middle East, in dishes such as *tabouleh*, lamb, yogurt, and *baharat* spice blend. In Asia, mint is mixed into curries and chutneys, rolled in to spring rolls, and floated in soups. Mint is a surprisingly pleasant accompaniment to spicy foods.

There are some interesting varieties available at garden centers and farmers' markets, with names that indicate their flavors, such as pineapple mint, licorice mint, chocolate mint, and orange mint.

Miso

See Appendix B.

MSG

Monosodium glutamate

Also known as *aji-no-moto*

This flavor-enhancing compound was discovered in the early twentieth century in kelp (*laminaria japonica*). After a large batch of *kombu* broth was evaporated, the remaining crystals had a meaty, savory taste now referred to as *umami*. The compound was isolated and identified as *glutamic acid*.

Tomatoes, cheese, and mushrooms all have high amounts of naturally occurring glutamate. It has no taste of its own, yet it somehow enhances flavor of other foods. It was shown to cause brain damage in lab mice, but theories differ on the danger to humans. Most agree that occasional use does not affect adults but may cause problems in young children.

MSG is available in supermarkets in a product called Accent and in Asian markets.

Mugwort

A member of the botanical family *asteraceae* (sunflowers)

Also known as *Saint Johns plant*

Considered a perennial weed, the silver fuzzy leaves and small yellow flowers of mugwort (*artemisia vulgaris*) were a traditional ale flavoring before hops came into common use.

The leaves and flowers have a flavor reminiscent of mint and juniper, and they work as a nice accompaniment to poultry, pork, and legumes, as well as stronger meats like lamb. Mugwort is also commonly used to flavor sweet Japanese rice cakes called *mochi*.

Find mugwort dried or in plant form on the Internet (blessedherbs.com).

Must

This is the name given to the juice of grapes which includes the seeds, skin and stems. In ancient Rome, must was boiled into a sweet syrup called *defrutum* or *sapa*, and used to preserve foods, and add a sour tannic flavor. The term must is commonly used to describe the flavor of certain spices and herbs.

Must is used in Greece (called *moustos*) for syrups and candies, but it is difficult to obtain, and typically made at home.

Mustard

A member of the botanical family *brassicaceae* (mustard, cabbage)

Mustard (*brassicaceae*) is the head of its own botanical family. Most kids know mustard as the yellow stuff in the squeeze bottle and are surprised to learn that it comes from a tiny seed.

There are several varieties of mustard that all look similar, with large green leaves and long stems topped with yellow flowers, but the long seed pods bear a variety of different seeds. White (*brassica sinapis alba*) and yellow (*brassica hirta*) produce large seeds that really pack a spicy punch. Black (*brassica nigra*) and brown (*brassica junicea*) are the most common forms and have a milder flavor.

The essential mustard oils are only released when the seeds are ground and mixed with water. (That's why mustard powder lasts so long in your pantry.) Any mixture made with ground mustard should be allowed to sit for 15 minutes to fully develop.

Major mustard production takes place in Dijon, France, where the main ingredient, besides mustard, is wine. England is known for its mustard powder. In Asia, mustard seeds are fried in oil until they pop, releasing their oil.

Leaves of the variety *brassica junicea* are grown as a vegetable. The flavor is similar to kale, with a mustard-horseradish flavor. It's a common ingredient in soul food, cooked with ham hocks, collards, and kale.

Mustard seeds are available at most supermarkets.

Homemade Herb Mustard

Once you see how easy making mustard is, you'll be hooked. Try making it with different spices and herbs, horseradish, or honey.

3 TB. yellow mustard seeds
3 TB. brown mustard seeds
½ tsp. caraway seeds
1 whole allspice berry
¼ tsp. white peppercorns
¼ tsp. salt
1 shallot, minced
½ tsp. fresh thyme, chopped
¼ cup white wine
¼ cup white wine vinegar

1. In a small coffee grinder, grind yellow mustard, brown mustard, caraway, allspice, and peppercorns to a fine powder. Transfer to a blender, and add salt, shallot, and thyme. Blend.

2. In a small bowl, combine wine and vinegar, and add to running blender very slowly. Continue to purée until mixture is a smooth paste. Store in a glass or plastic airtight container in the refrigerator.

Myrtle

A member of the botanical family *myrtaceae* (myrtle)

The head of its botanical family, the myrtle (*myrtus communis*) is a bushy evergreen shrub native to the Mediterranean region. Its pointed, shiny leaves carry a distinctive rosemary-bay fragrance. Both its leaves and its deep purple berries are used to flavor meats, similar to juniper berries.

M

Myrtles' long white showy flowers are a common addition to potpourri, and they add a peppery, floral flavor when tossed into fruit or green leaf salads. The wood makes an aromatic addition to the grill for curing, roasting, and smoking. The leaves dry well, and grinding them brings out a more peppery flavor.

Look for myrtle leaves on the Internet (silk.net/sirene).

Nam Pla

See Appendix B.

Nasturtium

A member of the botanical family *tropaeolaceae* (nasturtium)

Originally from Peru, the trailing, climbing vines of the nasturtium (*tropaeolum majus*) produce one of the most common edible flowers on the American plate. The large round flat leaves and yellow or orange flowers have a grassy, peppery taste that become popular in the 1970s, along with other organic, seasonal foods. The flowers make a lovely edible garnish and are equally at home stuffed with herbed cheese, creamed into butter, or fried in batter. The leaves can be wrapped around shrimp or filled with rice like grape leaves. Crushed with garlic and olive oil, the leaves make a nice, pestolike sauce, too. Not to leave them out, the flower buds can be picked and pickled like capers.

Nasturtiums are sometimes available at farmers' markets. They are easy to grow from seed, which are available at any nursery.

Nasturtium Salmon in Parchment

This classic cooking method is called *en papillote* in French, meaning "in paper." Parchment is sold in many supermarkets, but if you can't find it, foil works just as well.

2 shallots, minced
1 TB. fresh tarragon, minced
1 TB. fresh chervil, minced
1 TB. fresh parsley, minced
1 TB. fresh chives, minced
¼ cup nasturtium leaves and petals
Zest and juice of 1 small lemon
1 cup olive oil
4 (3-oz.) salmon fillets
1 TB. sea salt

1. Preheat the oven to 400°F.

2. In a large bowl, whisk together shallots, tarragon, chervil, parsley, chives, nasturtiums, and lemon zest and juice. Slowly add olive oil, whisking until well combined.

3. Lay each salmon fillet in the center of a large piece of parchment paper or aluminum foil. Distribute herb dressing evenly over each fillet.

4. Bring together the edges of the parchment paper up around fish and crimp together to seal tightly. Place packets on a baking sheet and bake for 15 minutes. Transfer packets to plates, and open at the table.

Natto

See Appendix B.

Nigella

A member of the botanical family *ranunculaceae* (buttercup)

Also known as *kalongi, black onion seed, Black cumin,* and *black caraway*

Nigella seeds (*nigella sativa*) have many confusing synonyms, but it bears no relation to any of them. Worse still, nigella seeds look a lot like black sesame seeds and are often used interchangeably. It's too bad, because the nigella seed gives off a musty, smoky flavor that none of the others have.

Swollen seed pods grow out of center of the flowers, which sit at the top of long stalks, with dill-like leaves and flowers that range from white, yellow, pink, blue, and purple. The flowers (known as love-in-the-mist) are popular with ornamental gardeners and are often seen whole as a garnish.

Nigella seeds are commonly used in Indian cuisine, in breads like *naan*, curries and korma, dahl, and in several spice blends.

Look for nigella at Indian markets.

Naan

This East Indian flat bread is used as a utensil alongside traditional curries. Made in a cylindrical clay tandoor oven, a flat circle of dough is slapped onto the side of the oven, giving it the tradional snowshoe shape.

1 pkg. active dry yeast

1 cup warm water

1 TB. sugar

¼ cup plain yogurt

1 TB. nigella

1 tsp. kosher salt

3 or 4 cups bread flour

2 to 4 TB. *ghee*

1. In a large bowl, combine yeast and warm water, and stir to dissolve. Add sugar, yogurt, nigella, and salt, and stir to combine. Add flour slowly, and stir until a firm dough forms.

2. Turn out dough onto a lightly floured surface, and knead for 8 to 10 minutes or until dough is smooth and elastic, adding more flour as needed. Cover dough with a warm, damp towel, and let rise until double in volume.

3. Divide dough into 8 portions and roll into balls. Pat balls flat into discs and elongate into ovals about ½ inch thick.

4. Preheat an iron skillet or griddle to high. Oil lightly with ghee, add dough, and cook for 2 to 4 minutes or until golden brown and puffy. Brush uncooked side with ghee, flip, and brown. Serve warm.

Chefspeak

Ghee is clarified butter in which all the moisture has been evaporated and the fat itself browns and takes on a nutty flavor. You can make it at home by slowly melting a pound of butter, carefully skimming off the foam, and pouring the pure fat off the sediment. This is clarified butter. Cook the clarified butter slowly until it turns a deep golden brown. Store ghee in the refrigerator for several weeks.

Nopales

A member of the botanical family *cactaceae* (cactus)

Also known as *prickly pear*

The large round flat pads, also known as stem segments, of the prickly pear cactus (*opuntia ficus-indica*) are a favorite ingredient in both Mexican and Mediterranean cuisines. Native to Mexico, the plant was brought back to Europe by Spanish explorers, where it now grows abundantly. Its prickly pear fruit is still consumed on both continents.

The spines need to be carefully removed from the stems with a knife or peeler, and the pads can be sliced thinly and used in recipes with seafood, eggs, vegetables, and salsas or eaten grilled with lime and olive oil.

Nopales are highly nutritious, with loads of vitamins, potassium, and iron. Take care when preparing, as excessive heat will create a slimy, okralike consistency.

Buy nopales at Latin American markets.

Nori

A member of the family *bangiaceae* (red algae)

(*Algae is technically neither a plant nor animal.*)

Also known as *kim*, *gim* in Korea, and *hăitái* in Chinese

Nori is the most familiar form of seaweed in the West. It's processed in the same way as paper, and the thin sheets are used to wrap sushi and rice balls. Nori is also shredded as a garnish for soups and vegetable dishes. It's commonly toasted and often flavored with soy sauce, sugar, and spices.

Buy nori at Japanese markets.

Nutmeg

A member of the botanical family *myristicaceae*

This tall evergreen tree (*myristica fragrans*) is native to the Indonesian Banda Islands, where the Portuguese first found it in the 1500s. The Dutch soon monopolized the nutmeg trade, displacing the natives and working the plantations with indentured slaves and convicts.

Today nutmeg grows throughout Indonesia, Madagascar, Grenada, and the Caribbean. The tree has long, thin leaves and tiny yellow flowers, similar to a peach tree. The fruit itself looks like a fig as it buds and a funny round pear when it's ripe. The juicy pulp hides a pit surrounded by a red fleshy net, or *mace*. Beneath the mace is a pit with a hard exterior shell. And inside the shell is the nutmeg. The nutmeg is soft when first removed, but becomes rock hard when dried in the sun. Mace is also dried in the sun, and the two are packaged and sold separately.

Historically, nutmeg was used as a mild sedative, and it's a common belief that taking large quantities will produce a hallucinogenic effect.

Nutmeg and mace share a similar flavor when ground. Mace is a bit stronger than the sweet, spicy nutmeg. Both are available whole and ground, but the flavor of the ground versions tends to dissipate rapidly. Special nutmeg graters are available for gadget-lovers, and they greatly extend the life of nuts. A grated nut will seal itself up after use, and very little of the flavorful oil will dissipate through the wound. Mace is equally long-lasting, although a bit more difficult to grind. I find that a mortar and some muscle work best for small amounts. Grind larger amounts of mace in a coffee grinder.

Nutmeg is commonly thought of as a sweet spice, but it's used in all sorts of savory recipes, too. French cuisine especially uses nutmeg in starch, grain, egg, and cheese dishes for just the right balance.

Whole and ground nutmeg is widely available in markets across the globe.

Onion

A member of the botanical family *liliaceae* (lily, onion)

There are many varieties of onion (*allium*), including leeks, shallots, chives, and garlic. They all share a similar structure, with hollow single stems growing out of bulbs and flowering into pom-pom flowers, and every part of the plant is edible.

The ancient Egyptians worshipped the onion, its concentric rings a symbol of eternal life. Onions are still prized for their different parts. Bulb onions have a round core expanding into layers, with a papery outer skin. They include the red or purple Bermudas, sweet Vidalia and Walla Wallas, common white and yellow, as well as round and elongated shallots (*allium oschaninii*).

Some alliums are valued for their stems. They do not have a rounded bulb, but instead grow a long cylinder of tightly packed leaves. These include the leek (*allium ampeloprasum*), the scallion or green onion, the Welsh onion (*allium fistulosum*), and the smallest of the species, the chive (*allium schoenoprasum*), which grows in clumps and includes the Japanese garlic chive *Ku chai*, (*allium tuberosum*). The greens and flowers can be harvested from all onions, regardless of their variety.

The pearl onion (*allium cepa*), or *walking onion* or *tree onion*, is a peculiar form. The plant grows a mass of bulbs at the top of the stem, where a normal onion flower would appear.

Onions are used in infinite ways, but certain preparation methods bring out different characteristics. Cut onions release more of their harsh oils than onions cooked whole. If onions are to be eaten raw, you can tame the harsh oils by thoroughly soaking and rinsing in cold water. Roasting whole or chopped and sautéed over slow heat brings out an onion's natural sugars, which can be further cooked to caramelization.

In addition to fresh, onions are also commonly available in dried, flaked, powdered, or salted forms, all processed from dehydrated bulbs. Be aware that these dried forms have a more concentrated flavor.

Onions are available wherever people like to eat.

Opal Basil

See Basil.

Orange

A member of the botanical family *rustaceae* (citrus)

Originally from China, the common sweet orange (*citrus sinensis*) is probably a hybrid of ancient pomelos and tangerines that grew wild throughout Asia. Like other citrus fruits, the orange comes from a tall tree with shiny, deep-veined tapered evergreen leaves and fragrant white flowers. Citrus trees were planted along trade routes by Portuguese, Spanish, Arab, and Dutch sailors to prevent scurvy. Ponce de Leon and Columbus planted trees in the new world.

There are several varieties and hybrids of orange, including the bitter Seville orange (*citrus aurantium*); the sweet Valencia, grown for its juice; and the navel, taken from an odd mutation of a Brazilian sweet orange and planted in Riverside, California. The blood orange, grown throughout the Mediterranean and more recently in California, contains streaks of red *anthocynin* pigment not usually found in citrus but common in other vegetables and flowers. Rumor has it that the orange was cross-pollinated with a rose. The mandarin orange (*citrus reticulate*) is smaller and sweeter than an orange and has loose skin.

The tangerine is a less-sweet variety of mandarin. The tangelo is hybrid of tangerine (mandarin) and pomelo. The pomelo (*citrus maxima*), also known as the *shaddock*, is the largest and oldest citrus fruit, native to Southeast Asia, where it grows wild on riverbanks. The pomelo tastes like a sweet, mild grapefruit and has a very thick peel, which is commonly used for candies and preserves. The grapefruit is hybrid of pomelo and orange and is named for the way the fruit clusters on the branch. Kumquats, which look like tiny oranges, are a separate genus, *fortunella*.

In the spice world, the orange is valued for its peel's aroma. The essential oils, once used by Chinese women to scent their hands by simply holding the fruit, add their aroma to foods of all kinds. It can be used fresh, grated or peeled from the fruit, chopped fine, infused in chunks, or dried and pulverized to a powder.

Orange flower water is the distillation of orange blossoms and is used in cocktails and baked goods. The flavor and aroma are floral, not citrusy, and are favored both in Middle Eastern and in recipes from the Victorian era.

Oranges are available everywhere. Find orange extract and oil in better supermarkets.

Oregano

A member of the botanical family *lamiaceae* (mint)

The same species and family as marjoram, oregano (*origanum vulgare*) grows taller, bushier, and hardier. The flavor is quite a bit stronger than that of marjoram, and the herb is used throughout the Americas, Italy, and Greece more than marjoram. Originally from the Mediterranean, for centuries oregano was used as an antidote for hemlock.

Oregano is one of the more pungent herbs. If tasted carefully, you can draw out hints of pepper, mint, and fennel. Oregano dries well, and if kept whole, it will retain its fragrance longer than most dried herbs. Powdered oregano has a much shorter life. When using fresh oregano, look for woody, bushy stems, and crush or rub it before adding it to a pot to release the flavorful oils.

Mexican or Puerto Rican oregano is another plant altogether (*lippia graveolens*, of the family *verbenaceae*). It's very similar to Mediterranean oregano, but because it's from the verbena family, it has more citrus essence.

Oregano is available fresh and dried at most supermarkets. Mexican oregano can be found in Latin American markets.

Pandan Leaf

A member of the botanical family *pandanaceae*

Also known as *screwpine*

Historically, the pandan tree (*pandanus amaryllifolius*) had many uses throughout the Pacific, including building and clothing material, dyes, medicines, as well as spiritual significance. But the fruity-rose essence of the flowers and the earthy, smoky-nut flavor of the leaves have made the pandan essential in the region's cuisines, where it's used as much as vanilla is in the West. Look for it cooked with chicken in Thailand, confectionery in Vietnam, and custards and rice in Bali and Malaysia. In addition to the unique flavor, pandan leaves impart a natural green color.

The leaves are best fresh, as they lose most of their flavor when dried. Fresh leaves are hard to come by outside the Pacific Rim. However, you can find pandan essence in a liquid form in Asian markets.

Pandan Coconut Rice

You can make this luscious green rice using 2 teaspoons pandan essence if don't have pandan leaves.

1 (5.6-oz.) can coconut milk
3 cups water
3 pandan leaves, knotted
1 tsp. fresh ginger, grated
2 TB. chives, minced
1 cinnamon stick
3 star anise
2 TB. sugar
1 tsp. kosher salt
1 tsp. black pepper
2 cups rice
½ cup peanuts, chopped

P

1. In a large saucepan, combine coconut milk, water, pandan leaves, ginger, chives, cinnamon stick, anise, sugar, salt, and pepper. Bring to a boil over high heat. At the boil, add rice. Stir, reduce heat to low, and cover.

2. Cook for 20 minutes or until liquid is absorbed. Serve warm, topped with chopped peanuts.

Paprika

A member of the botanical family *solanaceae* (nightshade)

The sweet red peppers (*capsicum annum*) used in the production of paprika are native to South America, but major production of paprika takes place in Hungary and Spain. There, they have elevated spice-making to an art form. More than simply ground sweet red peppers, real paprika is sweet and complex with a touch of heat.

How the peppers got to Hungary is not entirely clear. Turkish traders traveling between Portugal and Asia probably brought them. Regardless of how or why, the Danube region has become the only European region that eats chiles as an integral part of its cuisine. This is in no small part due to the perfect combination of soil, weather, rain, and sun the Szeged region of southern Hungary enjoys.

Specific grades of paprika all come from the same chiles. The flavor and heat are controlled by the degree of ripeness and the size of the pods when they're picked, which is directly related to the proportion of pepper wall to the seeds and inner membrane. The following table lists the common grades of paprika.

Paprika Grades		
Különleges	special quality	brightest red and most mild
Édes Csemege	delicate	mild with rich pepper flavor
Csemegepaprika	exquisite delicate	slightly spicier than delicate
Csipõs Csemege, Pikáns	pungent exquisite	hotter than delicate
Rózsa	rose	strong aroma, mild pungency, the most exported
Édesnemes	noble sweet	bright red, mild flavor
Félédes	half-sweet	a blend of mild and spicy
Erõs	hot	light brown, hottest of all paprika

The color of paprika ranges from pale orange to deep dark red, the brighter being the most mild. Real Hungarian and Spanish paprika has little in common with the red powder found in most American markets. Here, it's a blend of chile powder and cayenne, and it's used less for its flavor than its color.

In Hungary, paprika is the foundation of the national dish, goulash (*gulyás*, meaning "cattleman"), which, in its traditional form, is a brothy beef stew with vegetables and plenty of paprika. The paprika must be delicately fried to bring out just the right flavors without turning bitter.

Look for good-quality paprika at gourmet stores and specialty markets, or try the Internet (thespicehouse.com).

Paracress

A member of the botanical family *asteraceae* (sunflower)

Also known as *toothache plant*

Not a member of the cress family, paracress (*spilanthes acmella*) has large dark green leaves, red stems, and big yellow-red flower heads that look like the center of a daisy with no petals.

P

Native to Brazil, fresh paracress has a unique quality. At first taste, they're savory, almost mushroomlike. As it sits on the tongue, a warming sensation begins, triggering salivation and then tingling into numbness before dissipating. The unique qualities are often combined with other hot and spicy flavorings like garlic, chiles, and other peppers for a layered effect.

Paracress is rare outside Brazil but can be found in some online catalogues (www.koppertcress.nl).

Paracress Salsa

Serve this salsa to all your chile-loving friends. It will knock their socks off!

1 cup cilantro, chopped
¼ cup epazote, chopped
2 paracress flower heads, chopped
5 green onions, chopped
2 cloves garlic, minced
Zest and juice of 6 Key or Mexican limes
¼ cup olive oil
4 ripe tomatoes, diced
4 tomatillos, diced
1 cucumber, peeled and diced
2 jalapeño chiles, minced
2 poblano chiles, roasted and chopped
½ tsp. sea salt
½ tsp. black pepper

1. In a large bowl, combine cilantro, epazote, paracress, onions, garlic, and lime zest and juice. Stir together and slowly add olive oil.

2. Add tomatoes, tomatillos, cucumber, jalapeño chiles, poblano chiles, salt, and pepper. Toss to combine, and marinate at room temperature for 1 hour.

3. Taste and adjust seasoning with salt or lime as needed. Serve with tortilla chips.

Parsley

A member of the botanical family *umbelliferae* (parsley)

The two most common forms of parsley are the original flat Italian (*petroselinum neapolitanum*) and curly (*petroselinum crispum*). Flat parsley, which is slightly stronger in flavor, has small, flat, leaves clumped together on thin, tender stems that grow tall and flower into tiny pale yellow blooms. Curly parsley has ruffled leaves, and is commonly used as a garnish. Both types can be used fresh and dried, although much of the essence is lost in the later form.

Parsley is an essential ingredient in *tabbouleh*, the national dish of Lebanon; the French herb sachet *bouqet garni*; and the Italian condiment *gremolata*. Parsley has a high chlorophyll content, which gives food an herby flavor without the presence of heat, spice, or floral perfumes. Chlorophyll also makes parsley a natural breath freshener.

Another form of parsley (*petroselinum tuberosum*) is cultivated for its root, which can be eaten like a carrot, either fresh or cooked.

Parsley is available everywhere.

Beurre Maître d'Hôtel (Maitre D'Butter)

Serve this classic French spread on fish, beef, poultry, vegetables, potatoes, eggs, and bread.

1 lb. unsalted butter, softened to room temperature
¼ cup parsley, chopped
2 TB. shallot, minced
3 TB. lemon juice
¼ tsp. sea salt
¼ tsp. white pepper, ground

1. In a large bowl, beat together butter, parsley, shallot, lemon juice, salt, and pepper until well combined.

2. Spoon mixture onto a sheet of parchment or waxed paper, and roll into a log. Refrigerate until firm.

Pasilla

See Appendix C.

Pepper

A member of the botanical family *piperaceae* (pepper)

The pepper vine (*piper nigrum*) grows in tropical regions, close to the equator. In its natural jungle habitat, it climbs up trees 20 feet high. It has thick, broad, dark green leaves and small white flowers that grow in clumps. The flowers mature into berries that ripen from green to orange to red.

Tidbit

Pink peppercorns are actually a different species from white or black.

To produce black pepper, berries are harvested green and dried in the sun until wrinkled and black. White pepper is made from ripe berries that have had the skin removed before drying. Unripe green peppercorns are also sold in brine, still green and soft.

Pepper is one of the most popular spices in history. It was used in the embalming rituals of ancient Egypt, paid as taxes in ancient Rome, and the third-century cookbook *Apicius* uses pepper in nearly every entry. Let's not forget Vasco de Gama and his Portuguese mariners, who were inspired by pepper to find a route to India.

The finest pepper is produced in Southwest India, where the large berries are picked by hand off trellised vines. The flavor is more pungent than the stuff in the shaker on your table. It's higher priced, too.

Spicy and pungent, peppercorns can be added whole or ground for use in both savory and sweet dishes. They are commonly available.

Pineapple Pepper Ice Cream

The combination of spicy black pepper and sweet, acidic pineapple creates an explosion of flavor on your tongue. It's suprisingly refreshing.

½ pineapple, cut into large dice
2 TB. black peppercorns, crushed
½ cup brown sugar
1 vanilla bean, split and scraped
1½ cups heavy cream
1½ cups half-and-half
6 egg yolks
¾ cup sugar
½ tsp. kosher salt

1. Preheat the oven to 400°F.

2. In a large bowl, combine pineapple, pepper, brown sugar, and vanilla bean. Mix well, transfer to a baking sheet, and spread out into an even layer. Roast, stirring occasionally, until pineapple begins to brown, about 45 minutes. Transfer to a large bowl.

3. In a large saucepan, combine cream and half-and-half and bring to a boil.

4. In a medium bowl, whisk together egg yolks, sugar, and salt. Add ½ cup hot cream to yolk mixture, and whisk together quickly. Add yolks back to cream. Continue stirring over high heat until mixture is thick like a runny milkshake, about 2 or 3 minutes. Pour over roasted pineapple and cool completely.

5. Run cooled custard and pineapple through a blender, and strain out the chunks. Freeze in an ice-cream machine, following the manufacturer's instructions.

Pepper, Chile

See Chile Pepper.

Pepper, Pink

A member of the botanical family *anacardiaceae* (cashew)

The Peruvian (*shinus molle*) and Brazilian (*shinus terebinthifolius*) pepper trees are common ornamental trees in the warm climates of California, Florida, and the Mediterranean. The berries, while peppery in flavor initially, carry more of a sweet, juniper quality once bitten. They're commonly mixed with other peppercorns but then its flavor is lost. Try it on lighter foods, like fish and vegetables, where its subtleties can be appreciated. Add pink peppercorns at the end of the cooking, as excessive heat diminishes the flavor.

Dried pink peppercorns do not retain their flavor long. Look for the papery pink outer skin to be on the berry, and not at the bottom of the jar.

Pink peppercorns are available at better supermarkets.

Pink Peppercorn Biscotti

These twice-baked cookies were originally meant to be dipped in *vin santo,* a sweet Italian red wine. They are just as good dipped in coffee or milk, and this particular variation does well in Earl Grey tea.

2¾ cups flour
2 tsp. baking powder
¼ tsp. salt
1½ sticks butter
1 cup sugar
3 TB. pink peppercorns, crushed
Zest of 3 lemons, minced
1 egg
1 TB. milk

1. Preheat the oven to 350°F. Line 2 baking sheets with parchment paper.

2. In a medium bowl, sift together flour, baking powder, and salt, and set aside.

3. In a large bowl, using a sturdy spoon or an electric mixer, cream butter, sugar, peppercorns, and lemon zest until lump free. Add egg and milk. Slowly add sifted ingredients, and mix well to fully incorporate.

4. Roll dough into logs approximately 3 inches wide by the length of the baking sheet. Bake for 30 to 40 minutes or until golden brown and firm to the touch. Remove from the oven, and while warm, cut into ¾-inch slices using a serrated knife.

5. Return biscotti to the baking sheet and return to the oven. Bake for 5 to 10 minutes or until toasted. Flip cookies and toast other side for 5 to 10 more minutes.

Pepper, Sweet

See Sweet Pepper.

Pepper, White

See Pepper.

Peppermint

See Mint.

Perilla

A member of the botanical family *lamiacea* (mint)

Also known as *shiso, Chinese basil,* and *purple mint*

Native to Southeast Asia, this green pointed, jagged-edged leaf (*perilla crispa*) is most recognized as a sashimi and tempura garnish. A purple variety (*perilla altropurpurea*) is used for its red pigment (*anthocynin*) to dye pickled foods, including the pickled ginger on the side of your sushi. Purple perilla is sometimes mistaken for purple or opal basil.

The flavor is an interesting mix of mint, cinnamon, licorice, and citrus. The green variety sometimes tastes gingery as well.

Another perilla variety (*frutescens*) is grown for its oil and seeds, which are dried and used as a spice. The leaves lose their flavor easily when overcooked, so add them at the end of cooking or eat them fresh.

Perilla is available at Asian markets.

Mixed Berry-Perilla Compote

Use this decadent mixture to top ice cream, shortcakes, brownies, or lemon pie.

1 pt. blackberries
1 pt. raspberries
1 pt. blueberries
1 pt. strawberries, stems removed and cut in ½ or ¼
¼ cup purple perilla leaves, chopped
¼ cup sugar
Zest and juice of 1 lime
¼ tsp. kosher salt

1. Pick through, rinse, and air dry blackberries, raspberries, and blueberries.

2. In a large bowl, combine berries, strawberries, perilla, sugar, lime zest and juice, and salt, and toss to combine thoroughly.

3. Marinate at room temperature for 1 hour before serving.

Persillade

See Appendix B.

Pimiento

See Sweet Pepper.

Poblano

See Appendix C.

Ponzu

See Appendix B.

Poppy Seed

A member of the botanical family *papaveraceae* (poppy)

The same poppy from which the dangerously poisonous and addictive opium is derived (*papaver somniferum*) also produces the perfectly safe and flavorful seeds floating in your muffins, cakes, pastries, and candies. The white or pink flower gives way to a seed capsule that contains both the poisonous juice and the safe seeds.

The blue-black poppy seed is the most common, but a smaller, milder white version (*papaver somniferum album*) is sometimes seen in Indian cuisine. The poppy seed, with its nutty flavor, can be ground into a paste, and the white seeds can be ground to a flour and used as a thickener. Both seeds are used to fill pastries, including *mohn*, the filling for *hamentaschen* cookies.

Poppy seeds are high in oil and should be bought in small quantities as needed or stored in the refrigerator to prevent rancidity. Poppy seeds are very hard, and many recipes call for the seeds to be soaked in liquid to soften.

You can find poppy seeds in most supermarkets.

Poppy Seed Fruit Salad

This is a refreshing salad for hot summer days—or days you wish were hot.

½ cup orange juice
¼ cup raspberry vinegar
Zest and juice of 1 lime
3 TB. poppy seeds
¼ tsp. Szechwan pepper, ground
¼ tsp. anise seed, ground
¼ tsp. sea salt
¼ cup olive oil
1 banana, sliced into rounds
½ cantaloupe, diced
½ honeydew, diced
1 mango, diced
1 papaya, diced
2 kiwis, diced
1 pt. strawberries, rinsed, trimmed, and halved
2 cucumbers, peeled and diced

1. In a large bowl, whisk together orange juice, vinegar, lime zest and juice, poppy seeds, Szechwan pepper, anise, salt, and olive oil.

2. Add banana, cantaloupe, honeydew, mango, papaya, kiwi, strawberries, and cucumbers, and toss well to incorporate. Chill for 30 minutes before serving.

Quatre-Epice

See Appendix B.

Rakkyo, Rakyo

See Appendix B.

Ras el Hanout

See Appendix B.

Rock Salt

See Salt.

Rocket

A member of the botanical family *brassicaceae* (mustard)

Also known as *arugala*

This hearty annual (*eruca vesicaria*) thrives in hot, dry Mediterranean climates. Its large leaves and pale white flowers have a delicate, peppery flavor.

Rocket is used fresh as a vegetable in salads, chopped and added to soups and pastas, and crushed with olive oil and garlic like pesto. It's best used fresh or added to recipes at the end of cooking. Serve it on Valentine's Day, as it's a known aphrodisiac.

Rocket is available from specialty growers and at better farmers' markets.

Rose

A member of the botanical family *rosaceae* (rose)

The head of its own botanical family, the flowering rose (*rosa*) has long been used in the Middle East as a flavoring and was all the rage during the Victorian era. Roses are currently experiencing a surge in popularity. Floral additions to food, especially pastry, are popping up more and more.

The aroma come from the petals, and while the standard garden-variety roses work, the heirloom tea roses seem to provide the best flavor and most pungent aroma.

The petals can be steeped into recipes or packed in sugar to absorb their oils. Distilled rose water is an even easier way to add rose flavor to your favorite recipes.

Rose hips, classically used for jellies and teas, are the fruit of the rose plant. They appear as red, orange, or purple balls, left on the bush after the flower has died. Roses with opened-faced flowers produce the best hips, with a fruity, spicy, tart flavor, a little like rhubarb. The best hips are firm, not mushy or wrinkled. Remove the seeds and skin and dry or purée the inner pulp. Rose hips are a potent source of vitamin C.

Roses and rose hips are available from specialty growers, and rose hip tea is available at health food stores.

R

Rose Hip Applesauce

This dish is great on its own, spooned over fresh fruit and granola, or as a sweet accompaniment to roasted pork and lamb.

6 fuji apples, peeled, cored, and diced
2 cups rose hips, bud end removed
½ cup water
½ cup sugar
Zest and juice of 1 lemon
½ tsp. salt

1. In a large saucepan, combine apples, rose hips, water, sugar, lemon zest and juice, and salt. Place over medium heat and simmer, covered and stirring occasionally, until apples and rose hips are tender. Add more water during simmering if necessary.

2. Remove the pan from heat, and pass mixture through a food mill or purée in a food processor and then pass through a colander.

Rosemary

A member of the botanical family *lamiaceae* (mint)

Rosemary (*rosmariunus officinalis*) is one of the most familiar of all herbs, probably because it doesn't look like any of the others. Its evergreen leaves look just like pine needles, and its stalks, topped with tiny blue flowers, can grow quite tall. Throughout the Middle Ages, rosemary was considered an herb of fidelity and love and was worn as a wreath at weddings.

Rosemary's flavor is unmistakable. Its woody, pine-sage aroma can easily overpower a dish, so it's commonly paired with strong foods that can stand up to it, like gamey meats and winter vegetables. But in moderation, rosemary adds a delightful touch to sweet foods, too. Try it in apple pie, lemon scones, or vanilla sauce. Use the flowers for a salad garnish, or candy them as you would violets. The woody stalks make great smoke for the grill, and the twigs, peeled and soaked in water or wine, make aromatic skewers.

Rosemary is readily available in supermarkets, both fresh and dried.

Rue

A member of the botanical family *rutaceae* (citrus)

Also known as *garden rue*

Rue (*ruta graveolens*) is an evergreen shrub from the Mediterranean with a bitter citrus flavor that's used to balance flavors of foods as varied as cheese, spirits, and salads.

Its carrot top–like leaves and yellow flowers have long been believed to hold spiritual and medicinal properties, and during the Middle Ages, it was hung in doorways to keep evil spirits at bay. Some say the phrase *rue the day* comes from the Roman habit of throwing rue at an enemy.

In Ethipoia, rue is added to coffee and is an integral part of the national spice mix *berbere* (see Appendix B). The bitter flavor complements acidic foods like tomatoes, pickled vegetables, and olives, and it's a flavor component in both grappa and bitters.

Grow your own rue, or look for it on the Internet (mountainroseherbs.com).

Hot Stuff

Don't confuse *rue* with *roux*, the French thickening agent made of equal parts melted butter or fat and flour.

Olive Spread

Spread this on slices of crusty French bread.

3 TB. fresh rue, chopped fine
1 tsp. red wine vinegar
¼ cup olive oil
¼ cup Parmesan cheese
1 cup pitted kalamata olives, minced
1 cup pitted green Spanish olives, minced
1 clove garlic, minced
1 tsp. capers, minced

1. In a large bowl, mix together rue, vinegar, olive oil, and cheese. Add kalamata olives, green olives, garlic, and capers, and stir to combine.

2. Marinate at room temperature for several hours before serving.

Safflower

A member of the botanical family *asteraceae* (sunflower)

The low-cholesterol oil of the safflower (*carthamus tinctorius*), extracted from its seeds, is the most common use of this thistlelike herb today. But historically, it was grown as a dye, both for food and textiles. Its shaggy orange flowers look a lot like saffron to the uninitiated, so beware. Disreputable vendors have been known to try and fool the consumer. If you fall victim, you'll know right away, as the flavor of safflower is practically nonexistent.

Safflower threads are sold for dye and tea on the Internet, and in health food stores (mountainroseherbs.com).

Saffron

A member of the botanical family *iridaceae* (iris)

In the center of a low-growing purple crocus (*crocus sativus*) are three orange stigma. These stigma are the most cherished of all spices, saffron. Its exorbitant price is justified when you consider that the stigma must be picked by hand, and it takes approximately 75,000 stigma to make 1 pound saffron.

Luckily, it doesn't take much saffron to color and flavor your food. One or two strands, carefully steeped in liquid, can infuse a whole pot of rice with its dry, floral aroma. Nonbelievers soon discover that too much of a good thing is bitter and unpleasant.

Saffron is used throughout Europe and the Middle East. It's grown in India, Iran, and Spain, as well as Mexico. The Spanish government oversees a grading system, but no such system exists in Iran or India. Still, the quality is high, and connoisseurs can judge the quality, country of origin, and even territory by flavor and aroma.

Often the color is simulated by the use of turmeric, safflower, or marigold, but the sweet and pungent flavor cannot be duplicated.

When buying saffron, look for a vibrant red color. The older it gets, the closer to brown it becomes. Saffron is harvested in late fall, and good suppliers will date their product. Saffron keeps well, but don't pay too much for a batch that's obviously old. Old saffron is dry and brittle, so avoid a batch with a lot of broken pieces at the bottom of the jar.

Saffron is available at most fine supermarkets.

Russian Easter Bread (*Kulich*)

This bread is a celebration of spring, but it tastes great any time of year.

1 cup golden raisins
1 cup rum
1 cup milk, at room temperature
½ cup sugar
1 pinch saffron threads
1 (.25-oz.) pkg. active dry yeast
4 eggs
Zest of 1 orange
1½ sticks butter, softened to room temperature
2 tsp. salt
4 to 6 cups bread flour
1 egg yolk
¼ cup cream

1. In a small bowl, combine raisins and rum and soak overnight, or warm together in the microwave and set aside for 1 hour.

2. In a large bowl, stir together milk, sugar, saffron threads, and yeast. Set aside for 15 minutes or until bubbles begin to appear. Stir in eggs, orange zest, butter, salt, and raisins. Add flour slowly, and stir until a firm dough forms.

3. Turn out dough onto a lightly floured surface, and knead for 8 to 10 minutes or until smooth and elastic. Add more flour as needed. Cover dough with a warm, damp towel, and let rise until double in volume, about 2 hours.

4. Preheat the oven to 350°F.

5. Divide dough into three equal pieces, and roll each into a rope about 18 inches long. Braid ropes together into one loaf, and set on a buttered baking sheet.

6. Mix egg yolk and cream, and brush over the surface of loaf. Bake for 30 to 40 minutes or until golden brown. The loaf should sound hollow when thumped. Cool completely before slicing.

Sage

A member of the botanical family *labiatae* (mint)

Many varieties of sage grow wild wherever the climate is comparable to the Mediterranean. The most common culinary species (*salvia officinalis*) has a long woody stem, with silvery-gray-green leaves that are a little fuzzy, and purple flowers. The leaves can be used both fresh and dry. Rubbed sage, named for the method by which it is removed from the stem, is full of air, and should be used in greater quantity than fresh leaves.

Historically, sage has been an important medicinal herb. Its species name, *salvia*, is the Latin root of *salvation*. The herb has been known to cure everything from digestive disorders to sore throats, and was thought to promote longevity and improve the memory of the elderly. (If I'm remembering correctly.)

Sage is a common addition to Mediterranean and Middle Eastern cuisines. Its cedarlike aroma complements meats of all kinds, cheese, vegetables, and even fruits.

Sage is available fresh and dried in most supermarkets.

Salsify

A member of the botanical family *asteraceae* (sunflower)

Also known as *goatsbeard* and *oyster plant*

The root, shoots, flowers, and sprouted seeds of this showy purple wildflower (*tragopogon porrifolius*) originally from the Mediterranean are all edible. The root, often called oyster plant because of its flavor, is eaten as a vegetable and has a flavor akin to that of sun chokes or artichokes. The shoots have a similar flavor and are often steamed or tossed in vinaigrette. The seeds are sprouted and added to salads and sandwiches.

The root is available in better supermarkets and farmers' markets in the winter. Look for seeds online (yankeegardener.com) or in your nursery to start a crop in your garden.

Salt

Sodium chloride

Easily the most important addition to any pantry, salt not only flavors food, but also plays a vital role in human existence by regulating the water content in the body. More important, salt enables us to preserve food, making us less dependent on seasonal availability and able to wander from our homes for extended periods of time. It enabled early civilizations to move about the globe, discovering one another. Salt was our ticket to ride.

Salt was historically a hot commodity, difficult to obtain and, therefore, quite expensive. It can be harvested from sea water or rock deposits left from ancient seas. From the ocean, salt water is dried by the sun in shallow pools. Mined salt (*halite*), also known as rock salt, grows in isometric crystals and is very hard.

Several types of edible salt are commonly available. Table salt is usually iodized. Potassium iodide is added as a dietary supplement to preventing iodine deficiency, a major cause of goiter and cretinism. Most table salt has a water-absorbing additive to keep it from clumping, and some countries add fluoride as well.

Many chefs prefer kosher salt, which gets its name from its use in the koshering process of meats. Koshering requires that all fluids be extracted from an animal before it is consumed. The larger crystals dissolve more slowly, extracting more fluids from the meat. Kosher salt has no additives, which gives it a cleaner, less-metallic taste.

Fleur de sel ("salt flower") is natural sea salt, hand harvested and gourmet priced. It usually comes from specific locations, most notably off the coast of Brittany, in France. Each location produces distinct flavors due to the area's naturally occurring vegetation and minerals. Sea salt removed from the top layer of water is pale and delicate in flavor, while gray sea salt, which is allowed to sink and mix with the ocean water, is more robust in flavor.

You might also find black salt, gray salt, pink salt, smoked salt, marsh salt, and even moon salt (harvested at night, not from the moon). You can spend quite a lot of money on salt, but beware: once it's mixed into foods, the unique character of these specialty salts is easily lost. Reserve their use for applications in which you'll notice it.

Get your pricey salt at gourmet markets or on the Internet (saltworks.us).

Salted Figs with Chocolate and Almonds

This dish makes an exquisite after-dinner sweet. Serve it with strong coffee or a glass of port.

2 TB. almonds, toasted and ground
1 (8-oz.) bittersweet chocolate bar, chopped or grated into fine chunks
16 dried black mission figs
2 tsp. fleur de sel or other coarse sea salt

1. Preheat the oven to 350°F.

2. In a small bowl, mix together almonds and chocolate.

3. Insert your thumb into the bottom of each fig (opposite the stem end), making a pocket. Stuff each fig pocket with almond-chocolate mixture, and set stuffed figs on a baking sheet. Bake at 350° for 10 minutes or until warmed through.

4. Place warm figs on a serving platter, and sprinkle each with a pinch of salt. Serve immediately.

Sambal

See Appendix B.

Sansho

See Szechuan Pepper.

Santa Fe

See Appendix C.

Sassafras

> A member of the botanical family *lauraceae* (laurel)
>
> Also known as *gumbo filé* and *filé powder*

This North American tree (*Sassafras albidum*) with mitten-shaped leaves was first appreciated for the flavor of its bark. The roots, saplings, and leaves were boiled and steeped into a root beer–flavored tea.

Native American tribes were the first to discover the thickening power of the sassafras leaf. Today the leaf is dried and powdered and available as *filé*. This thickener has a slight root beer–camphor flavor. It should be used sparingly, as it's very powerful. If too much is added too soon to a recipe, the result is a thick, gluey paste. Add it at the end of cooking, off the heat, and let the residual heat thicken and flavor your pot.

Filé powder is available at most supermarkets. Look for sassafras bark on the Internet (worldspice.com).

Savory

> From the botanical family *lamiaceae* (mint)

You can find several varieties, both annual and perennial, of savory (*satureja*). Summer savory is more delicate in flavor and has a shorter growing season. Winter savory is the stronger of the two and can be used for prolonged cooking with stronger flavors.

The leaves of this short plant have a peppery flavor, similar to rosemary and thyme. It's an important ingredient in several spice blends and is commonly used to flavor legumes and meat stuffing throughout northern and eastern Europe and Canada.

You can grow your own savory, or look for it from specialty growers at your farmers' market. Seeds are available at most nurseries.

Toasted Almonds with Savory and Garlic

These nuts are as at home at a classy cocktail party as they are at a casual football party.

2 TB. olive oil
3 cloves garlic, minced
¼ cup fresh savory, minced
1 lb. almonds, whole, raw, skin-on
¼ cup kasseri cheese

1. Preheat the oven to 350°F.

2. In a small saucepan, heat olive oil and add garlic. Sauté over high heat until garlic begins to color. Remove from heat, add savory, and set aside.

3. Spread almonds out on a baking sheet and toast for 8 to 10 minutes or until fragrant. Remove nuts from the oven and toss with oil mixture and cheese. Serve warm.

Scallion

See Onion.

Scotch Bonnet

See Appendix C.

Sereh

See Lemongrass.

Serrano

See Appendix C.

Sesame Seed

A member of the botanical family *pedaliaceae*

Also known as *goma* and *benne seeds*

Originally from North Africa, the sesame seed (*sesamum indicum*) comes from an annual plant with long bushy leaves and white or purple tubular flowers.

Both white and black seeds are commonly available, and both share a rich nutty flavor that's greatly improved by toasting. The seed is full of oil, which is used extensively throughout the world. Sesame oil has a short shelf life and should be bought in small quantities or stored in the refrigerator to prevent rancidity.

A common form of sesame is *tahini*, a paste used in Arabic and Greek cuisine. It's added to recipes, served as a spread and condiment, or sweetened for candy. The Japanese have a similar sesame paste called *neri-goma*. Sesame seeds are often also combined with honey in confectionery.

Benne is the Nigerian name for the seeds, and they are considered lucky in West Africa. Slaves brought them to the United States, and sesame seeds remain a popular baking ingredient throughout the South. The rest of the country knows them more commonly as a topping for breads, either on their own or mixed with other seeds.

Sesame seeds are widely available.

Sesame Brittle

This is a sweet-spicy treat. If you're not into heat, omit the cayenne.

1 cup sesame seeds
1½ cups sugar
½ cup corn syrup
⅓ cup cold water
3 TB. butter
1 tsp. salt
¼ tsp. baking soda
½ tsp. vanilla extract
½ tsp. cayenne

1. Preheat the oven to 200°F. Lightly butter a large sheet of waxed or parchment paper and set aside.

2. Spread sesame seeds on a baking sheet and keep warm in the oven while sugar boils.

3. In a large saucepan, combine sugar, corn syrup, and water, and bring to a boil. At the boil add butter, and cook to 300°F on a candy thermometer (hard-crack stage). Remove from heat, and add salt, baking soda, and vanilla extract. Stir until foamy, and immediately fold in warm sesame seeds and cayenne.

4. Quickly transfer to prepared wax paper and spread out as thin as possible. Cool completely and then break into pieces. Store in an airtight container at room temperature.

Shallot

See Onion.

Shiso

See Perilla.

Shoga

See Ginger.

Sichuan

See Szechuan Pepper.

Silphium

A member of the botanical family *apiacea* (parsley)

Also known as *silphion* and *laser*

This is an ancient variety of giant fennel—or so we think, because most agree that it's now extinct.

To the ancient Greek costal city of Cyrene, in what is now Libya, silphium was a crucial source of wealth. So revered was the herb that its image was depicted on their coins. As you might imagine, it was valued as a food, eaten like fennel is today, from the root to the seed. But this alone didn't make it popular. It was silphium's medicinal properties that made it the rock star of herbs. The resin extracted from its stalk was a reliable contraceptive, strictly regulated and exported across the ancient world.

Alas, the herb was difficult to propagate, and it was soon overharvested into extinction.

Sofrito

See Appendix B.

Sorrel

A member of the family *polygonaceae* (knotweed)

Also known as *sheep's sorrel* and *field sorrel*

The leaves of this perennial plant (*rumex acetosa*) are shaped like an arrow, and its spikes of red flowers make it one of the more recognizable weeds. Its rhizome can easily take over a field. Happily for food lovers, the leaves have a fresh acidic flavor, similar to a kiwi fruit. It's a welcome ingredient in salads, soups, and sauces. The sour bite sharpens the flavor of other ingredients and stimulates the appetite, much like vinaigrette. Additionally, juice from the leaves will curdle milk and has been used historically in place of rennet for cheese-making.

Jamaican red sorrel is an unrelated hibiscus, used in jellies and teas (it's the red in *red zinger*). Its flavor is very close to that of common sorrel and has often been used as a tart substitute for cranberry juice.

Sorrel is available at better supermarkets and farmers' markets. Red sorrel is available as a dried herb in ethnic markets.

Iced Sorrel

This is zingy-er than anything you can buy.

1 cup chopped fresh sorrel
¼ cup dried Jamaican sorrel
1 cinnamon stick
2 or 3 star anise
¼ cup brown sugar
Zest and juice of 1 Mexican lime
6 cups boiling water
2 or 3 cups ice

1. In a large saucepan, combine fresh sorrel, Jamaican sorrel, cinnamon stick, star anise, brown sugar, lime zest and juice, and water. Bring to a boil, remove from heat, and steep for 15 minutes. Strain into a large pitcher and add ice.

2. Chill, and serve over ice.

Spearmint

See Mint.

Spice *Parisienne*

See Appendix B.

Star Anise

A member of the botanical family *illiciaceae*

This small evergreen tree (*illicium verum*) native to China produces small yellow flowers; large, thick leaves; and star-shape fruit. This fruit, which contains hard shiny seeds, has a potent anise flavor. The flavor of both anise seed and star anise comes from the compound anethol, but the two plants are not botanically related.

The fruit has more flavor than the seeds, although both are packaged together in bits and pieces. Higher grades of star anise can be had for a price, but the grades are based on appearance only and have no effect on flavor. Finding a star intact with all its seeds in place is considered very good luck.

Star anise is a component of *Chinese five-spice powder* and a common addition many dishes, both savory and sweet.

Star anise is available in most supermarkets and Asian grocers.

Sumac

A member of the botanical family *anacardiaceae* (cashew)

This wild shrub (*rhus coriaria*) grows throughout Sicily, southern Italy, and Iran. Its clusters of tiny red berries are prized for their sour, astringent taste. Sun-dried and shriveled, sumac is ground into a purple powder and used to flavor meat for grilling, stews, rice, and sauces. It's an important ingredient in the Arabic spice blend *za'atar* (see Appendix B).

If you're using whole berries, be sure to soak them to soften before grinding.

Look for sumac at Middle Eastern markets or online (nirmalaskitchen.com).

Sumac Lamb Kebabs

Kebab means "skewer of roasted meat," and similar dishes are found throughout Eastern Europe, the Middle East, and Asia. Both metal and wooden skewers work fine, but be sure to soak wooden ones in warm water for at least 30 minutes so they won't ignite.

3 cloves garlic, minced

1 TB. fresh ginger, grated

1 TB. dried thyme

2 tsp. dried chile powder (such as ground dried New Mexico Chiles)

¼ cup sumac, ground

½ tsp. allspice, ground

1 tsp. kosher salt

3 lb. lamb leg or loin, trimmed and diced into 2-in. cubes

1. In a large zipper bag, combine garlic, ginger, thyme, dried chile powder, sumac, allspice, salt, and lamb. Seal the bag and toss to mix ingredients. Marinate in the refrigerator for 12 to 24 hours or overnight.

2. Preheat the grill to high heat.

3. Remove meat from marinade and discard marinade. Thread meat onto skewers, and grill, turning every 4 or 5 minutes, until desired doneness, about 15 minutes for medium-rare. Serve with yogurt and rice.

Sweet Pepper

A member of the botanical family *solanaceae* (nightshade)

Also known as *bell pepper*

Native to the tropical regions of the Americas, sweet peppers (*capsicum annuum, grossum group*) are like chile peppers in most ways, except the leaves and fruits are larger and the seeds are not spicy. The annual bushes produce fruits that ripen from green to all shades of red, yellow, orange, and purple.

Sweet peppers are eaten as vegetables, adding color to dishes such as soups, stews, salads, and pasta. Their flavor changes when roasted or grilled, adding charred, smoky flavor to recipes. Pimientos are roasted sweet red peppers that have been skinned, seeded, and preserved.

Like chile peppers, sweet peppers can be dried and ground into powder or preserved in brine.

Sweet peppers are commonly available at most markets.

See also Chile Pepper and Paprika.

Szechwan Pepper

A member of the botanical family *rutaceae* (citrus)

Also known as *sichuan pepper, fagara,* and *flower pepper*

This prickly ash tree (*zanthoxylum piperitum*) native to China bears no relation to peppers or chiles. The tiny berries' red outer pods are prized in cuisines throughout Asia. The flavor is tart and citrusy with a peppery numbness, similar to that of clove. The inner black seeds are bitter and should be avoided. Szechwan pepper is an ingredient in *Chinese five-spice powder.*

A related tree, the Japanese prickly ash, *sansho* or *kinome* (*zanthoxylum sancho*) is prized for its leaves as well as its buds.

Szechwan pepper is available at Asian markets.

Szechwan Pepper Melons

Try this refreshing snack by the pool on the hottest of hot days. Dice everything either large or small, but all the same size.

1 cup lime juice
1 tsp. sea salt
2 TB. Szechwan pepper
1 cup honeydew melon, peeled and diced
1 cup cantaloupe melon, peeled and diced
1 cup watermelon, peeled and diced
1 cup jicama, peeled and diced
1 mango, peeled and diced
1 cucumber, peeled, seeded, and diced

1. In a large bowl, stir together lime juice, salt, and Szechwan pepper. Add honeydew, cantaloupe, watermelon, jicama, mango, and cucumber, and toss together.

2. Marinate in the refrigerator for 30 minutes before serving.

Hot Stuff

You can peel a mango with a peeler, but I have an easier method: cut both halves off the center pit and use an extra large spoon to scoop out, like you would an avocado. The fruit can then be easily diced or sliced.

T

Tabasco

See Appendix C.

Tahini

See Sesame; Appendix B.

Tamari

See Appendix B.

Tamarind

A member of the botanical family *fabaceae* (bean)

Also known as *tamarindo, sampaloc,* and *Indian date*

Tamarind is a sticky brown pulp found inside a fuzzy brown bean pod. The pods are found on a tropical evergreen tree (*tamarindus indica*) originally from East Africa and grown now throughout Sudan, Madagascar, India, and Mexico. It's a huge tree, growing easily over 50 feet tall. Its bright green leaves are feathery, and the yellow flowers look like orchids.

Sweetened for candy or salted and dried into snacks, the tart pulp is as popular worldwide as lemons are in the West. It plays a prominent role in Philippine *adobo,* Indian *sambar,* and *pad thai* from Thailand. In Mexico, it's used to make candy and sweet beverages. (*Tamarind* is the nickname given to the traffic cops of Mexico city— because of their uniform color, not their fuzzy, lumpy shape.) Tamarind is a key ingredient in Worcestershire sauce, English brown sauce, and western barbecue sauce.

Purchase tamarind pods whole at Asian or Mexican markets, or find the pulp in brick form, with or without seeds. Steep the pulp in liquid and strain out the hard seeds before using.

Refreshing Tamarind Punch

This refreshingly tart drink is common south of the border. Make it a special treat at your next pinic or barbecue.

¼ cup tamarind pulp
½ cup sugar
8 cups water
1 mango, peeled and diced
2 oranges, sliced
1 pt. strawberries, trimmed and halved

1. In a large pitcher, combine tamarind pulp and sugar. Add water, and stir to blend. Add mango, oranges, and strawberries.

2. Chill for 30 minutes before serving over ice.

Tarragon

A member of the botanical family *asteraceae* (sunflower)

A native of Central Europe, tarragon (*artemisia dracunculus*) can be identified by its smooth and narrow, pointed leaves that look like grass growing up a thin stem.

The flavor is a pleasant, peppery anise, and used fresh and young it will perfume a dish wonderfully. Tarragon is favored in French cuisine and finds its way into many of the classic spice blends, as well being the backbone of *sauce béarnaise* (tarragon-infused hollandaise).

Tarragon doesn't dry well but is commonly preserved in oils and vinegars. You can also chop and freeze it in ice cubes or zipper bags. Its tiny green flowers are too pungent for most palettes.

Mexican tarragon is a separate species (*tagetes lucida*) with the same flavor.

Fresh tarragon is available at better supermarkets.

T

Tasmanian Pepper

A member of the botanical family *winteraceae* (winters bark)

Also known as *mountain pepper*

The berries, flowers, and leaves of this tree (*tasmania lanceolata*) are used in cuisines of the Southern Hemisphere, including Australia, New Zealand, and throughout the Pacific Rim.

Unrelated to black pepper, the taste of the dried berry is at first sweet, then spicy, then numbing. The leaves are dried and used like bay, with similar heat and a hint of citrus. When ground, the leaves have a thickening power similar to sassafras.

Tasmanian pepper is an integral component of Australian cuisine, commonly found in meat marinades. It's not readily available outside the country but can be ordered online (www.atasteofthebush.com.au).

Tasmanian Marinade

This is a great marinade for red meat and game. For sea-food and poultry, replace the red wine with white, omit the Worcestershire sauce, and add some lime juice.

2 tsp. Tasmanian pepper, crushed

4 cloves garlic, minced

2 bay leaves, crushed

1 TB. Worcestershire sauce

1 tsp. kosher salt

2 cups dry red wine

2 cups olive oil

4 (6-oz.) beef or lamb steaks or chops

1. In a large bowl, combine Tasmanian pepper, garlic, bay, Worcestershire sauce, salt, wine, and olive oil. Mix well, and add meat. Marinate for 6 to 12 hours.

2. Preheat the grill to high heat.

3. Remove meat from marinade and discard marinade. Grill meat to desired doneness.

Thai Chile

See Appendix C.

Thyme

A member of the botanical family *lamiaceae* (mint)

There are more than 300 species of thyme (*thymus*), a low perennial shrub with twiggy stems, tiny oval leaves, and little white or pink blossoms. Many thyme plants are grown as a fragrant ornamental ground cover, but its usefulness in the kitchen cannot be overlooked.

Thyme is a standard ingredient in all Mediterranean and Middle Eastern cuisines. It's an important ingredient in several spice blends, including *Bouquet Garni, Herbes de Provençe, Za'atar,* and *Jerk* (see Appendix B).

One reason for thyme's popularity is that its flavor is strong and long lasting. *Thymol,* the main flavor compound, can be found in many other herbs. It holds up well to prolonged cooking and drying, and it complements all foods, sweet and savory.

Several interesting varieties of thyme can be found with distinctive aromas, indicated by the names, including caraway thyme, lavender thyme, mint thyme, oregano thyme, coconut thyme, lime thyme, and lemon thyme. With the exception of lemon, which is fairly common at farmers' markets, you should be able to find these unique species through specialty growers (mountainvalleygrowers.com).

Tiger Lily Bud

See Lily Bud.

Tonka Bean

A member of the botanical family *fabaceae* (bean)

Also known as *tonquin* and *tonqua*

The bean of this South American legume tree (*dipteryx odorata*) has a distinctive vanilla flavor, with some spicy cinnamon, clove, and almond undertones. It's used frequently in perfumes, soaps, potpourri, and incense and was for years a component of pipe tobacco. Because of its spicy-nutty nature, tonka is sometimes used as a substitute for *mahlab* or *bitter almond.*

But tonka beans are rarely seen as a vanilla substitute because it contains high levels of *coumarin,* a lethal anti-coagulant, also found in woodruff. You can reduce the amount of this compound by soaking the bean in alcohol and then allowing fermentation.

The beans are produced in Venezuela and Nigeria, but the Food and Drug Administration (FDA) has banned them for use as a food product in the United States. If you're daring, you can find them through online auctions for use in witchcraft and perfumery.

Turmeric

A member of the botanical family *zingiberaceae* (ginger)

It's obvious that turmeric (*curcuma domestica*) is related to ginger. It grows in knobby rhizomes and has a similar gingery flavor with a hint of pepper heat. But once you cut into a turmeric root, it's clear you don't have ginger. The flesh inside is bright yellow-orange, and that pigment lends its color to many foods, including curry powder, cheese, butter, pickles, and hot dog mustard.

Powdered turmeric is made from the smaller offshoots of the main rhizome that are boiled, peeled, dried, and ground. Turmeric is available fresh, but its flavor is no more remarkable than the easily attained powder. Both forms will stain your skin and clothes, so take care.

Curcumin, the main flavor component and a powerful antioxidant, is being studied for its possible beneficial effects on Alzheimer's disease, cystic fibrosis, colon cancer, breast cancer, and melanoma.

Turmeric is widely available at most supermarkets.

T

Pineapple Chutney

This is a great accompaniment to spicy curries, or spread it over cream cheese for an exotic appetizer spread.

1 large pineapple, peeled, cored, and diced small
1 large purple (Bermuda) onion, minced
2 cups brown sugar
2 cups cider vinegar
1 TB. Dijon mustard
Zest and juice of 1 orange
Zest and juice of 1 lime
1 TB. ground turmeric
1 cup pitted dates, chopped fine
1 cup zante currants
1 mango, peeled and diced fine
2 bananas, peeled and diced fine

1. In a large saucepan, combine pineapple, onion, and brown sugar. Bring to a boil, stirring, reduce heat to a simmer, and add vinegar, Dijon mustard, orange zest and juice, lime zest and juice, and turmeric. Simmer, covered, for 1 hour, stirring occasionally, until thick.

2. Remove the pan from heat, add dates and currants, cool to room temperature, and chill for 2 hours or overnight.

3. Just before serving, stir in mango and bananas.

Vanilla

A member of the botanical family *orchidaceae* (orchid)

Vanilla comes from a perennial climbing orchid (*vanilla planifolia*) from South America. Its white flowers are followed by long, green pods that have been treasured for centuries. The Aztecs used it to flavor their *xocolatl* (bitter water). The Spanish brought the beans to Europe, where it became all the rage.

The French tried unsuccessfully to propagate vanilla on the Islands of Bourbon (now Reunion) and Madagascar in the Indian Ocean. As it turns out, the orchid had been naturally pollinated by bees and hummingbirds only found in Mexico. To make matters more difficult, the orchids themselves open for only a short time. But where there's a will, there's a way. Vanilla orchids grown outside of Mexico are now hand-pollinated, which, combined with their complicated processing procedure, guarantees their high price.

When the green, unripe pods are picked they have little flavor or aroma. Not until they are cured and fermented do they emit the familiar fragrance. *Vanillin* is the flavor compound that we love, and on fine beans it can be seen on the surface as white dust.

You can find three vanilla beans on the market. Madagascar beans are used mainly for extract production. Tahitian beans have a nice aroma but less flavor and are used mainly for perfumes. Mexican beans are fat and fragrant. The extract from Mexico may sometimes contain *coumarin*, a substance from the *tonka bean* that is banned in the United States.

Look for beans that are thick and tough but pliable. To use vanilla beans, pound them first before splitting them lengthwise to crush the millions of inner mini-seeds and activate as much oil as possible. Once scraped, spent pods can be stored in sugar or steeped in rum to harness as much of the oil as possible.

Most people use vanilla in its extract form. It's made by macerating the vanilla beans in alcohol. Beware of Mexican vanilla extract, as it's often made with banned *tonka beans*. Vanilla paste, which is concentrated extract with added seeds, has become popular in recent years. There's also vanilla powder, which is dried, ground pods. Imitation vanilla is much weaker than the real thing. You can make vanilla extract at home by storing beans and spent pods in rum. Or store them in granulated sugar to absorb every bit of oil and then use the sugar in recipes for a vanilla essence.

V

Vanilla extract and beans are available at most markets. Look in better stores for better-quality extracts. Beans are expensive, but several online sources offer fair prices (thespicehouse.com, vanilla.com).

Aztec Hot Chocolate

This red-hot chocolate milk will warm your insides, to say the least.

6 dried pasilla chile pods
4 cups boiling water
1 qt. half-and-half
2 cinnamon sticks, crushed
1 lb. bittersweet chocolate, chopped fine
3 vanilla beans, split and scraped

1. Preheat the oven to 400°F.

2. Spread chile pods on a baking sheet and toast for 5 minutes or until soft. Cool, remove stems, and seeds (be careful of the capsicum). Cover chile pods with boiling water, and steep for 30 minutes.

3. In a large saucepan, combine half-and-half and cinnamon sticks. Simmer over medium heat for 5 minutes and remove from heat. Add chocolate and vanilla beans, and stir to melt.

4. Transfer soaked chiles to a blender. Blend until smooth, adding chocolate mixture slowly as needed. Combine chile paste with remaining chocolate mixture, stir, strain, and re-warm before serving.

Verbena

See Lemon Verbena.

Violet

A member of the botanical family *violaceae*

Violets (*viola odorata*) are native to Europe, Asia, and North Africa. They are recognized by their heart-shape, fuzzy-bottomed leaves and five-petal purple flowers, two of which have a fuzzy yellow beard. Violets have long been treasured for their fragrance, beauty, and healing power. Violet petals are high in vitamin C and were once worn on the head in garlands to prevent headaches.

Violet leaves and petals have a fragrant, nutty flavor and make a nice addition to salads and soups. The flowers are a favorite for candying and are crystallized to decorate confections. Dried petals are infused into tea and syrup and used to make pudding and jelly.

Look for violets at farmers' markets, or grow your own (canyoncreeknursery.com).

Violet Granita

Serve this refreshing summer dessert in chilled glasses so it doesn't melt too quickly.

2 cups violet petals
4 cups water
1 cup sugar
1 TB. lemon juice
¼ tsp. kosher salt

1. In a large saucepan, combine violet petals, water, sugar, lemon juice, and salt. Bring to a boil, remove from heat, and cool completely. Strain into a shallow baking dish and place in the freezer.

2. Use a fork to mix up ice crystals every 20 minutes until the entire pan is frozen and slushy, about 2 hours. Serve over sliced peaches or berries.

V

Wasabi

A member of the botanical family *brassicaceae* (mustard)

Also known as *Japanese horseradish*

The wasabi root (*wasabia japonica*) looks like the trunk of a tiny palm tree. It grows naturally in riverbeds and cool mountain streams, but its production in Japan is pretty secretive. Consequently, unless you're eating at high-end sushi bars, most wasabi in the United States is actually horseradish dyed green.

Unlike horseradish, it's the inner core of wasabi that's the most potent. The fresh root is either shredded very fine or dried and powdered. Like mustard, the vapors of wasabi burn the nasal passage, not the tongue, a shocking revelation to wasabi newcomers.

Real wasabi paste dries and loses flavor very quickly and is, therefore, served between the fish and rice on sushi to keep it moist and prevent evaporation.

Wasabi-joyu is a combination of wasabi and soy sauce, used for dipping sushi and sashimi. Wasabi leaves are eaten in salads or batter-fried in tempura. They have a similar but milder flavor.

Look for wasabi root, powdered, paste, or fresh at Japanese markets.

Wasabi Potato Salad

This chilled salad comes with a kick. If you're not very heat-tolerant, cut the wasabi in half.

2 lb. red new potatoes
1 tsp. salt
1 tsp. wasabi, fresh grated, paste, or powder with 1 tsp. water
1 tsp. honey
1 clove garlic, minced
1 small purple (Bermuda) onion, minced
¼ cup cilantro, chopped
¼ cup rice vinegar
1 tsp. sesame oil
1 cup olive oil
2 stalks celery, chopped fine
6 to 8 red radishes, chopped fine
2 cups Napa cabbage, shredded

1. In a large pot, boil red potatoes in salted water until tender. Drain, cool, and slice into quarters. Set aside.

2. In a large bowl, whisk together wasabi, honey, garlic, onion, cilantro, rice vinegar, and sesame oil. Slowly add olive oil while whisking. Add potatoes, celery, radishes, and cabbage, and toss together to combine.

3. Chill for 30 minutes before serving.

Watercress

See Cress.

Wintergreen

A member of the botanical family *ericaceae* (heather)

Also known as *eastern teaberry* and *boxberry*

The wintergreen (*gaultheria procumbens*) is in the same family as the cranberry, blueberry, and huckleberry. The small evergreen shrub has tapered oval leaves, white bell-shaped flowers, and red berries. The leaves have a minty compound, *mentyl-salicylate*, which is the natural oil of wintergreen. Before the advent of chewing gum, wintergreen leaves were chewed as a breath freshener. The berries are also used as flavoring for desserts and beverages.

Wintergreen is also a natural source of *triboluminescence*. When dried and mixed with a hard substance like sugar, it builds up an electrical charge. When the asymmetrical crystal bonds are broken, scratched, or rubbed, an electrical charge builds and generates light. Because wintergreen oil is fluorescent, it turns ultraviolet light to blue light. If you happen to be in the dark, you'll see this as blue sparks.

Fresh and dried wintergreen is hard to find—unless it's growing in your yard—because it's currently endangered in several states and parts of Canada. Wintergreen oil is available at some health food stores.

Woodruff

A member of the botanical family *rubiaceae* (bedstraw)

Also known as *wild baby's breath* and *sweet scented bedstraw*

The white starry flowers, tall stems, and successive parasol-like leaves of woodruff (*galium odoratum*) are all dried and used for teas, liqueurs, and potpourri. Its sweet scent, a combination of mown hay and vanilla, comes from *coumarin*, the same substance found in *tonka beans* and banned in the United States for its anti-coagulant properties. Unlike the tonka bean, woodruff contains a relatively small amount of coumarin.

Woodruff grows wild in the shady woods of Germany's Black Forest region. There, it's used abundantly in sausages, preserves, and traditional May Wine.

Woodruff is available on the Internet dried (comfycountrycreations.com) and in seed form (seeds.ca).

May Wine

On May 1, celebrate spring the German way with this traditional wine punch.

1 cup fresh woodruff, roughly chopped
1 pt. strawberries, washed, trimmed, and quartered
1 pt. raspberries
¼ cup sugar
1 bottle white Moselle or Rhine wine
2 cups sparkling water

1. In a large bowl, combine woodruff, strawberries, raspberries, and sugar. Toss together, and set aside at room temperature for 30 minutes to marinate.

2. Add wine and sparkling water, and stir to combine. Serve over ice.

Wormwood

A member of the botanical family *asteraceae* (sunflower)

Also known as *absinthe wormwood* and *grand wormwood*

Native of Europe, Asia, and North Africa, this perennial shrub (*artemisia absiuthium*) gets quite a lot of attention. That's because the fuzzy silver stems, carrotlike leaves, and yellow bell flowers contain *thujone*, a chemical compound blamed for the supposed hallucinatory effects of *absinthe*, a highly alcoholic distilled spirit flavored with many herbs, including *anise* and wormwood.

W

Wormwood's flavor is fairly bitter, but it was coveted for its medicinal effects by the ancient cultures of Egypt and Greece. It's used against tapeworm, rheumatism, gout, and the common cold, as an anesthetic, and an appetite stimulant. It has a fever-reducing effect and repels moths and fleas. Pure wormwood oil is very poisonous and can cause convulsions, coma, and death.

Wormwood plants are available in nurseries throughout the spring and summer.

Yarrow

A member of the botanical family *asteraceae* (sunflower)

Also known as *milefolium* and *woundwort*

Native to Europe, yarrow (*achillea millefolium*) was believed to heal wounds and stop the flow of blood, and Achilles carried it into battle to treat his soldiers on the battlefields of Troy.

Yarrow grows in California, China, and anywhere gardeners want butterflies. Its fuzzy feathery leaves and flat pods of flower clusters spring up on a single stem from perennial rhizomes.

Yarrow's sweet, slightly bitter, sage-flavored leaves are eaten as a vegetable, fresh or cooked like spinach. Its flower heads are used to flavor wines, spirits, and tea. Medieval brewers used yarrow in an herbal mixture called *gruit*, which was used to bitter beer before hops were used.

Yarrow is available at most nurseries and on the Internet in tea form (kalyx.com).

Za'atar, Zahtar

See Appendix B.

Zedoary

A member of the botanical family *zingiberaceae* (ginger)

Also known as *white turmeric*

Native to India and Indonesia, zedoary (*curcuma zedoaria*) was known in sixth-century Europe. Its pink rhizomes have a musky, mango flavor, and are used in perfumes and spirit distillation.

Like ginger, zedoary can be grated and used fresh, or dried and used as a powder. If you chew it fresh it will turn your spit yellow. In powder form it is a common addition to pickles and curries, and the rhizome itself is often pickled as a condiment.

Look for zedoary in Indian and Asian markets and on the Internet (spiceworld.uk.com).

Zest

Exocarp

Zest is the outermost rind, or *exocarp* of citrus fruit. The outer colorful skin contains the essential oils and flavor compound that flavor the fruit itself and add strong citrus flavor to foods.

Zest from all the citrus fruits is used in sweet and savory recipes of all kinds. Additionally, zest can be cooked in sugar and eaten as candy, or peeled, dried, pulverized, and added as a spice.

Avoid the white pith underneath the zest but outside the fruit pulp. It's bitter.

Z

Appendix A

Glossary

absinthe A distilled spirit flavored with herbs, most notably wormwood. Prohibited in many countries based on rumors of psychedelic and addictive properties, absinthe has recently been allowed back in to some European countries.

amaretto An Italian liqueur with the distinctive flavor of bitter almonds.

annual A plant that germinates, flowers, and dies within a single growing season.

anthocyanin Red and blue pigments that occur in the plant kingdom.

aquavit A Scandinavian distilled spirit flavored with herbs and spices, most commonly caraway.

biennial A plant that takes up to 24 months to complete its life cycle.

boba An Asian beverage made originally with sweetened black tea, condensed milk, and large tapioca pearls, which sit at the bottom of the cup and drinkers suck up through oversize straws. Variations include fruit flavors.

botulism A potentially fatal foodborne illness, caused by ingestion of the nerve toxin *botulin*, most commonly occurring from improperly canned foods.

bouquet garni   An aromatic sachet of herbs and spices used in all kinds of classic French stocks, stews, and soups. The classic preparation uses a wilted leek green to wrap a bay leaf, parsley stem, thyme sprig, 3 peppercorns, and a clove. Today, the ingredients are often wrapped in cheesecloth. The bundle is tied with a long piece of kitchen twine and secured to the pot handle for easy removal.

brown sauce   A malt vinegar–based condiment flavored primarily with tamarind and Worcestershire sauce, popular in the United Kingdom. Elsewhere in the world, the term refers to a meat-based sauce or gravy, thickened with flour or roux.

capsaicin   The compound found in chiles that gives them their fiery heat (see Appendix C).

coumarin   A chemical compound found in plants, including the *tonka bean* and *woodruff*. It is commonly found as a flavorant in artificial vanilla and pipe tobacco. It has been banned as a food additive in the United States because it's considered mildly toxic to the kidneys.

dal, dahl   An Indian dish made from dried beans (*pulses*), often puréed and served alongside curry.

E. coli   This bacterium (*Escherichia coli*) is naturally occurring in the human intestinal tract, but certain strains can cause serious gastrointestinal distress, and in some cases, death. It is most commonly caused by undercooked meats and cross-contamination.

exocarp   The botanical name for the tough outer skin of fruit.

fish sauce   A liquid condiment and ingredient similar in appearance to soy sauce. Popular in Asia, fish sauce was known in ancient Rome.

foie gras   A French delicacy, foie gras is the enlarged liver of a goose or duck.

frankincense   This ancient aromatic resin from the *boswellia* tree is prized for its aroma and used in perfume and incense.

game meat   Game meat comes from animals who are wild, or were historically wild, such as venison, rabbit, buffalo, and bear. The term *gamey* refers to the strong flavor of the meat.

ghee   A clarified butter used in Indian cuisine in which all the moisture has been evaporated and the fat itself browns and takes on a nutty flavor.

grow light   These electric lamps produce light specifically to encourage photosynthesis. Spectrums of light can be adjusted to benefit the plant throughout its lifecycle.

gruit   An herb mixture used to add bitterness and flavoring to beer before the common use of hops.

hamentaschen, hamentash, oznei haman   This Ashkenazi cookie, which is shaped like a tri-corner hat, is eaten during the Jewish holiday of Purim. It is classically filled with a sweetened poppy seeds, but it is also seen with dried fruit, jams, and chocolate.

injera   A spongy, pancakelike Ethiopian bread, used as a utensil to scoop up the traditional spicy stews.

julienne   A thin, matchstick-size knife cut, typically ⅛-inch thick, used for many different foods.

legume   A plant with long seed pods containing beans or seeds, such as lentils, peanuts, and soybeans.

macerate   To soak food, usually fruit, in liquid to infuse flavor.

mirepoix   A blend of aromatic vegetables used in stocks, soups, and stew. Typically, the mix consists of carrot, onion, and celery sautéed in butter.

mortar   A bowl, usually made of ceramic or stone, into which spices, herbs, vegetables, and pharmaceuticals are put to be crushed by a pestle, a hard instrument shaped like a small baseball bat.

Moselle   Dry white wine produced along the Moselle River in Southwest Germany, made from *Riesling* and sometimes *Traminer* grape varieties.

mukhwas   Brightly colored, sugar-coated seeds, usually fennel, anise, and sesame, served in India as an after-dinner digestive aid and breath freshener.

myrrh This dried resin from the *commiphora* tree has been used for perfume and incense since ancient times and was worth as much as gold. Today, it's also used in skin ointments and some distilled spirits.

paneer This fresh, un-aged Indian cheese is similar in consistency and taste to fresh mozzarella.

panella A fresh, un-aged Mexican cheese, fairly bland and firm, similar to paneer.

perennial A plant that lives for several years, perennials may possess woody stems, bulbs, or rhizomes.

pulse The dried seeds of beans and peas, also called *legumes*.

rancidity A foul odor and taste of spoiled oil, or products containing oil, brought about by exposure to light and heat. Refrigeration prevents it.

Rhine wine Several varieties of dry white wine produced in the German Rhine River Valley.

rhizome Although often confused with a root, a rhizome is actually a bulbous, underground stem that grows horizontally at the surface of the soil.

sweet anise Another name for *fennel* bulb, although the actual herb *anise* is unrelated to fennel.

tandoor Used in Indian cuisine, this cylindrical clay charcoal oven cooks food at extremely high temperatures, retaining moisture, flavor, and nutritional benefits.

tapioca A starch extracted from the root of the cassava plant. Ground into flour or formed into pearls, it is used as a thickening agent.

thujone This chemical, found in *wormwood* and other herbs, has been blamed for supposed hallucinatory effects of the distilled spirit *absinthe*. Recently, however, it has been determined that the thujone does not induce hallucinations.

thymol This aromatic chemical compound is the main constituent in the oil of *thyme*.

tomatillos This small, acidic green fruit with a paperlike husk is commonly mistaken for green tomatoes, but is in fact closely related to the gooseberry.

triboluminescence This phenomenon of light generation occurs when certain hard crystal substances are broken or scratched.

vanillin This is one of the organic compounds responsible for vanilla flavor and is the main component of vanilla extract.

zante currants These tiny raisins are made from dried miniature seedless grapes.

Appendix B

Spice Blends and Condiments

The following list of spice blends and condiments are meant to get you started on your global culinary journey. There are thousands of other blends and condiments, for food and drink, from every country in the world. And there are hundreds of variations on most of the blends I've included here. Every region, spice vendor, family, and cook has a different interpretation of these mixes, and that's just fine. It's what makes cooking interesting.

Spice Blends

There are three basic methods of mixing spice blends: simply stirring ingredients together; stirring and then grinding; and stirring, toasting, and grinding. Stirring, you know about. There's not much expertise I can add to that.

Grinding isn't that hard either, but I have a few tips that might make it easier for you. I prefer to use a coffee grinder. It's small, which forces the spices through the blade more often than a larger food processor or blender does, producing a finer, more even grind. I recommend you get a separate grinder just for spices. I have had some mighty weird-tasting coffee after a particularly spicy kitchen escapade.

When I'm feeling historic, I enjoy grinding in a mortar. The result is rougher but more satisfying. There's also a method the French call *mignonette* in which you crush whole spices with the flat bottom of a frying pan. Don't whack the pan onto the spices like a fly swatter, but rather use the pan to knead or rub the spices into submission. This is typically done with pepper, but in a pinch, it works for everything.

Toasting is a vital stage in cooking with spices. Heat releases the spice oils, which changes their flavor, usually for the better. Use a dry pan, preferably made of iron, as it conducts heat evenly. Add the spices to the pan, and keep them moving by shaking the pan or stirring. This constant movement ensures the spices toast evenly. As soon as they become fragrant, the toasting is done. Be careful, as these tiny seeds and berries can burn very quickly. Remove them from the heat *and the pan*. Remember, the pan is still hot and it keeps cooking the spices until you remove them.

Hot Stuff

Cool the spices before you grind them. They are easier to handle, and they emit fewer fumes.

There are blends in the following pages that are not toasted first because the recipes they're typically used in call for the ground spices to be toasted in oil. And some blends simply do not benefit from toasting, such as the *Sweet Spices Mix* for baking.

Sometimes the toasting is done in stages, giving each ingredient in the blend the perfect cooking time to release its maximum flavor. But when we're talking about blends of 10 to 20 spices and herbs—who has that kind of time? Just keep in mind that small particles of spice cook faster than large ones. If your mixture includes a powder, either add it to the pan last, or watch that powder carefully while it cooks and use it as an indication of doneness for the rest of the mix.

Tidbit

The names of these blends can be intimidating, but don't let a lot of consonants scare you away. To get authentic flavor, you need the authentic spice blends, but you don't have to pronounce them correctly. And yes, I have called these recipes *spice* blends, even though they contain herbs. I use the term *spice* as an adjective and a verb here, because I want to help you *spice* up your life.

Baharat (North Africa)

This powder is fried to release its oils before being used in recipes. It's a common flavoring for meats in Lebanon, Syria, Jordan, and Israel.

¼ cup paprika
3 TB. black peppercorns
3 TB. coriander seed
3 TB. cumin seed
1 TB. allspice
1 TB. cardamom
1 TB. dried red chiles
1 TB. dried mint
1 tsp. clove
1 tsp. nutmeg
2 cinnamon sticks

1. In a small bowl, combine paprika, black peppercorns, coriander seed, cumin seed, allspice, cardamom, dried red chiles, dried mint, clove, nutmeg, and cinnamon sticks.

2. Grind to a fine powder using a coffee grinder.

Barbecue Rub (USA)

Rub this blend on beef, pork, or poultry and then marinate 6 to 12 hours prior to slow cooking over open fire. It can also be used as barbecue sauce seasoning.

½ cup chili powder
½ cup garlic powder
½ cup onion powder
½ cup cumin seed
½ cup dried oregano
½ cup dried thyme
¼ cup kosher salt
¼ cup celery seed
¼ cup black peppercorns
¼ cup yellow mustard seed
¼ cup paprika
2 TB. whole cloves
2 TB. cayenne

1. In a small bowl, combine chili powder, garlic powder, onion powder, cumin seed, dried oregano, dried thyme, kosher salt, celery seed, black peppercorns, yellow mustard seed, paprika, whole cloves, and cayenne.

2. Grind to a fine powder using a coffee grinder.

Variation: For Barbecue Sauce, combine 1 cup Barbecue Rub with 1 cup brown sugar, 1 cup tomato sauce, ¼ cup tamarind paste, and 3 tablespoons cider vinegar.

Berbere (Ethiopia)

This blend is essential to authentic Ethiopian food. It's used on meats and combined with onions and oil for use as a curry paste.

¼ cup ginger
¼ cup cumin
¼ cup coriander
¼ cup cardamom
¼ cup fenugreek
¼ cup paprika
2 TB. allspice berries
2 TB. red chiles
2 TB. nutmeg
2 cinnamon sticks
1 TB. kosher salt

1. In a small bowl, combine ginger, cumin, coriander, cardamom, fenugreek, paprika, allspice berries, red chiles, nutmeg, cinnamon sticks, and kosher salt.

2. Toast in a dry skillet, and grind to a fine powder using a coffee grinder.

Bouquet Garni (France)

Dangle this packet of herbs in soups and stocks to infuse the essence of France. The twine makes it easily removable and keeps spent herbs from clouding your creation.

1 sprig parsley
1 sprig thyme
1 sprig marjoram
1 bay leaf
3 peppercorns
1 whole clove

1. Wrap parsley, thyme, marjoram, bay leaf, peppercorns and clove in a wilted leek leaf or cheesecloth sachet and tie with kitchen twine.

2. Toss in your favorite soup or stock.

Cajun Spice (USA)

Use this spiced-up mix when you feel like a taste of the Big Easy.

1 cup bay leaves
1 cup paprika
¼ cup dried thyme
¼ cup dried oregano
¼ cup yellow mustard seed
¼ cup white peppercorns
¼ cup onion powder
¼ cup garlic powder
2 TB. cumin seed
2 TB. celery seed
2 TB. cayenne

1. In a small bowl, combine bay leaves, paprika, dried thyme, dried oregano, yellow mustard seed, white peppercorns, onion powder, garlic powder, cumin seed, celery seed, and cayenne.

2. Grind to a fine powder using a coffee grinder.

Chili Powder (USA)

Combine this mix with chopped or ground meat for chili. It also makes a great barbecue rub.

½ cup each paprika
½ cup dried red New Mexico chiles
½ cup cumin
¼ cup each garlic powder
¼ cup onion powder
¼ cup dried oregano
¼ cup dried thyme
2 TB. sesame seed
2 TB. allspice berries
2 TB. kosher salt
3 cinnamon sticks

1. In a small bowl, combine paprika, dried red New Mexico chiles, cumin, garlic powder, onion powder, dried oregano, dried thyme, sesame seed, allspice berries, kosher salt, and cinnamon sticks.

2. Grind to a coarse powder using a coffee grinder.

Chinese Five-Spice Powder (China)

This blend is commonly used to flavor duck, chicken, pork, and fish.

¼ cup black peppercorns
2 TB. fennel seed
8 star anise
1 tsp. whole cloves
2 cinnamon sticks

1. In a small bowl, combine black peppercorns, fennel seed, star anise, cloves, and cinnamon sticks.

2. Toast in a dry skillet before grinding to a fine powder using a coffee grinder.

Chaat Masala (India)

Chaat means "to lick," and this tangy blend makes you lick your lips, thanks to the amchoor. It's suitable as a topping for everything from curries to fruit salads.

¼ cup black peppercorns

3 TB. cumin seed, dried mint

2 TB. amchoor

2 TB. mint

2 TB. kosher salt

1 TB. cubeb pepper

1 TB. ajwain

1 TB. ginger

1 TB. asafetida

1 TB. cayenne

1. In a small bowl, combine black peppercorns, cumin seed, dried mint, amchoor, mint, kosher salt, cubeb pepper, ajwain, ginger, asafetida, and cayenne.

2. Toast in a dry skillet before grinding to a fine powder using a coffee grinder.

Char Masala (India)

This toasted blend is a common ingredient of Indian and North African rice dishes.

2 TB. cumin seed

1 TB. cardamom seed

1 tsp. allspice

1 crushed cinnamon stick

1. In a small bowl, combine cumin seed, cardamom seed, allspice, and cinnamon stick.

2. Toast in a dry skillet before grinding to a fine powder using a coffee grinder.

Corning Spice (Great Britain)

Use this blend for pickling and preserving meat or vegetables.

½ cup coriander seed

½ cup red chiles

½ cup mustard seed

½ cup bay leaves

¼ cup white peppercorns

¼ cup celery seed

¼ cup allspice berries

¼ cup grated ginger

2 cinnamon sticks, crushed

1. In a small bowl, combine coriander seed, red chiles, mustard seed, bay leaves, white peppercorns, celery seed, allspice berries, grated ginger, and cinnamon sticks.

2. Wrap mixture in a cheesecloth sachet, and use to infuse brines or vinegars.

Curry Powder (India)

Each region of India has its typical curry spice blends, and each cook within that region has his or her own interpretation of those blends. What's more, Indian spices are rarely premixed in India like they are here. This is a very generalized blend.

¼ cup coriander seed
¼ cup cumin seed
¼ cup brown mustard seed
3 TB. turmeric
3 TB. fenugreek
3 TB. black peppercorns
2 TB. ground ginger
2 TB. cardamom seed
1 TB. dried chiles
2 cinnamon sticks

1. In a small bowl, combine coriander seed, cumin seed, brown mustard seed, turmeric, fenugreek, black peppercorns, ground ginger, cardamom seed, dried chiles, and cinnamon sticks.

2. Grind to a coarse powder using a coffee grinder.

Dukka (Egyptian)

Use this spice blend when cooking meats, or mix it with olive oil as a dip for bread.

¼ cup sesame seed
¼ cup hazelnuts
¼ cup coriander seed
3 TB. cumin seed
3 TB. black pepper
3 TB. dried thyme
1 TB. kosher salt

1. In a small bowl, combine sesame seed, hazelnuts, coriander seed, cumin seed, black pepper, dried thyme, and kosher salt.

2. Toast in a dry skillet before grinding to a fine powder using a coffee grinder.

Fines Herbes (France)

Sprinkle these chopped fresh herbs onto seafood, poultry, stews, soups, vegetables, or salads.

Fresh chopped parsley
Fresh chopped chervil
Fresh chopped chives
Fresh chopped tarragon
Fresh chopped marjoram (optional)
Fresh chopped savory (optional)
Fresh chopped burnet (optional)

1. Combine equal amounts of chervil, chives, tarragon, marjoram, savory, and burnet.

2. Mix well.

Fish Boil (USA)

Use this blend to flavor boiling liquid for crab, shrimp, lobster, and crayfish. It can also be ground into a fine powder and added to soups, stews, and seafood dishes like shrimp salad or crab puffs.

1 cup sea salt
1 cup paprika
1 cup celery seed
1 cup bay leaves
3 TB. allspice berries
3 TB. white peppercorns
3 TB. yellow mustard seed
3 TB. grated ginger root
2 TB. cayenne pepper
2 TB. whole cloves
1 TB. cardamom seed
2 cinnamon sticks
1 whole nutmeg, crushed

1. In a small bowl, combine sea salt, paprika, celery seed, bay leaves, allspice berries, white peppercorns, yellow mustard seed, grated ginger root, cayenne pepper, cloves, cardamom seeds, cinnamon sticks, and nutmeg.

2. Mix well.

Garam Masala (Indian)

Garam means "warm" or "hot," but this is not a spicy hot. Rather, it makes you feel warm after you've eaten it. Also, it's toasted prior to grinding.

1 cup bay leaves
½ cup cumin seed
¼ cup coriander seed
3 TB. black pepper
3 TB. cardamom seed
3 TB. cloves
3 TB. ground nutmeg

1. In a small bowl, combine bay leaves, cumin seed, coriander seed, black pepper, cardamom seed, cloves, and nutmeg.

2. Toast in a dry skillet before grinding to a fine powder using a coffee grinder.

Gâlat Dagga (Tunisia)

This 5-spice blend is commonly used for Arabic stews.

¼ cup black peppercorns
¼ cup cloves
3 TB. grains of paradise
3 TB. grated nutmeg
1 cinnamon stick

1. In a small bowl, combine black peppercorns, cloves, grains of paradise, nutmeg, and cinnamon stick.

2. Grind to a coarse powder using a coffee grinder.

Gomashio (Japanese)

This simple combination tops Japanese rice dishes of all kinds.

¼ cup sesame seed
1 TB. sea salt

1. In a small bowl, combine sesame seed and sea salt.
2. Toast in a dry skillet.

Herbed Pepper (USA)

This is a nice change of pace for vegetables and meats.

¼ cup white pepper
¼ cup black pepper
1 TB. thyme
1 TB. savory
1 TB. oregano
1 TB. rosemary

1. In a small bowl, combine white pepper, black pepper, thyme, savory, oregano, and rosemary.
2. Mix well.

Herbes de Provençe (France)

This classic blend can be made with fresh or dried versions of these herbs.

¼ cup chervil
¼ cup marjoram
¼ cup tarragon
¼ cup basil
2 TB. thyme
2 TB. lavender

1. In a small bowl, combine chervil, marjoram, tarragon, basil, thyme, and lavender.
2. If fresh, mince all ingredients together. If dry, simply stir.

Italian Spice Mix (Italy)

Use this seasoning blend in sauces, sausages, vegetables, or as a marinade rub.

¼ cup fresh chopped oregano
¼ cup fresh chopped basil
¼ cup ground fennel seed
2 TB. fresh chopped sage
2 TB. fresh chopped rosemary
3 cloves garlic, minced

1. In a small bowl, combine oregano, basil, fennel seed, sage, rosemary, and garlic.
2. Mix well.

Jerk (Jamaica)

Use this traditional blend to marinate turkey, chicken, fish, or pork.

½ cup ground allspice
½ cup dried thyme
½ cup fresh grated ginger
½ cup fresh minced garlic
½ cup fresh minced onion
½ cup brown sugar
3 TB. ground coriander
3 TB. ground nutmeg
2 TB. ground clove
2 TB. kosher salt
2 cinnamon sticks, crushed
1 or 2 scotch bonnet peppers, minced
½ cup vegetable oil
½ cup rum

1. In a small bowl, combine allspice, dried thyme, ginger, garlic, onion, brown sugar, coriander, nutmeg, clove, kosher salt, cinnamon sticks, scotch bonnet peppers, vegetable oil, and rum.

2. Mix well.

3. Add meat and marinate 2 or 3 hours, or overnight, before cooking.

Kala Masala (India)

Kala means "black," and that's an apt description of the color and flavor after this blend has been toasted.

1 guajillo chile
¼ cup black pepper
3 TB. cardamom seed
3 TB. cumin seed
2 TB. shredded coconut
2 TB. nutmeg
2 TB. cloves
1 TB. anise seed
1 TB. poppy seed
1 TB. sesame seed
1 TB. turmeric
1 TB. amchoor
5 bay leaves
2 cinnamon sticks

1. In a small bowl, combine guajillo chile, black pepper, cardamom seed, cumin seed, coconut, nutmeg, cloves, anise seed, poppy seed, sesame seed, turmeric, amchoor, bay leaves, and cinnamon sticks.

2. Toast in a dry skillet before grinding to a fine powder using a coffee grinder.

Khmeli Suneli (Georgia)

This blend is used in Georgia and throughout the Caucuses with slow-braised stews of mutton, beef, or chicken.

¼ cup dill seed
¼ cup fenugreek
¼ cup dried marjoram
¼ cup bay leaves
3 TB. coriander seed
3 TB. dried peppermint
3 TB. celery seed
3 TB. dried parsley
2 TB. turmeric
2 TB. dried savory
2 TB. dried basil
2 TB. dried thyme
2 TB. black peppercorns

1. In a small bowl, combine dill seed, fenugreek, dried marjoram, bay leaves, coriander seed, dried peppermint, celery seed, dried parsley, turmeric, dried savory, dried basil, dried thyme, and black peppercorns.
2. Grind to a fine powder using a coffee grinder.

Mulled Wine Spice (Europe)

Steep this blend in a full-bodied red wine and simmer for 30 minutes.

2 TB. anise seed
2 TB. allspice
2 TB. cardamom
2 TB. fresh grated ginger
1 tsp. whole cloves
2 cinnamon sticks
Zest of 1 orange

1. In a small bowl, combine anise seed, allspice, cardamom, ginger, cloves, cinnamon sticks, and orange zest.
2. Mix well.
3. Wrap mixture in a cheesecloth sachet.

Panch Phoran (India)

This Bengali 5-spice powder is fried in oil to release flavors and then added to lentils, beans, potatoes, and fish.

2 TB. fenugreek
2 TB. nigella seed
2 TB. yellow mustard seed
2 TB. fennel seed
2 TB. cumin seed

1. In a small bowl, combine fenugreek, nigella seed, yellow mustard seed, fennel seed, and cumin seed.
2. Grind to a fine powder using a coffee grinder.

Quatre-Epice (France)

These four spices were traditionally combined for the ancient French spice bread, *pain d'epice.*

2 TB. white pepper
2 TB. nutmeg
2 TB. cinnamon
2 TB. ginger
Whole cloves (optional)

1. In a small bowl, combine white pepper, nutmeg, cinnamon, ginger and cloves (if using).

2. Grind to a fine powder using a coffee grinder.

Ras el Hanout (North Africa)

This is a Moroccan mix whose name means "top of the shop." There's no specific recipe, but it's the spice merchant's best blend.

¼ cup cardamom seed
¼ cup allspice berries
¼ cup cumin seed
¼ cup coriander seed
3 TB. dried chile pods
3 TB. black peppercorns
3 TB. cubebs
3 TB. grains of paradise
2 TB. whole cloves
2 TB. grated nutmeg
2 TB. rose petals
2 TB. grated galangal
2 cinnamon sticks

1. In a small bowl, combine cardamom seeds, allspice berries, cumin seed, coriander seeds, dried chile pods, black peppercorns, cubebs, grains of paradise, cloves, nutmeg, rose petals, grated galangal, and cinnamon sticks.

2. Toast in a dry skillet before grinding to a fine powder using a coffee grinder.

Salt Substitute (USA)

This is for those who need to watch their sodium intake.

1 TB. cayenne
1 TB. onion powder
1 TB. garlic powder
1 TB. dried savory
1 TB. dried thyme
1 TB. dried oregano
1 TB. dried sage
1 TB. nutmeg
1 TB. crushed black pepper
Grated zest of 1 lemon

1. In a small bowl, combine cayenne, onion powder, garlic powder, dried savory, dried thyme, dried oregano, dried sage, nutmeg, crushed black pepper, and lemon zest.

2. Mix well.

Hot Stuff

Be sure to use garlic and onion powder, not garlic and onion salt, which would defeat the purpose of a salt substitute.

Sambar Podi (Indian)

This powder is used for *sambar*, a Southern Indian soup that's also served over rice as an accompaniment to curry.

1 cup *chana dal* (small split chickpea)
¼ cup cumin seed
¼ cup coriander seed
¼ cup black peppercorn
¼ cup crushed red chiles
1 TB. turmeric
1 TB. amchoor
1 TB. turmeric
1 tsp. asafetida
1 cinnamon stick, crushed

1. In a small bowl, combine chana dal, cumin seed, coriander seed, black peppercorn, red chiles, turmeric, amchoor, turmeric, asafetida, and cinnamon stick.

2. Toast in a dry skillet before grinding to a fine powder using a coffee grinder.

Spice *Parisienne* (France)

This is a typical French blend, used as a rub on meats or to flavor stews, soups, and vegetables. It also goes by the name *épices fines*, which means "fine spices."

2 TB. black peppercorns
2 TB. white peppercorns
2 TB. crushed bay leaves
1 TB. sea salt
1 TB. grated nutmeg
1 TB. dried thyme
1 TB. ground ginger
1 tsp. whole cloves
2 cinnamon sticks

1. In a small bowl, combine black peppercorns, white peppercorns, bay leaves, sea salt, nutmeg, dried thyme, ginger, cloves, and cinnamon sticks.
2. Grind to a coarse powder using a coffee grinder.

Spiced Salt (USA)

Use this blend on meat, fish, and root vegetables before roasting or grilling.

1 lb. kosher salt
¼ cup black pepper
¼ cup coriander seed
¼ cup bay leaves
¼ cup whole cloves
¼ cup dried basil

1. In a small bowl, combine kosher salt, black pepper, coriander seed, bay leaves, whole cloves, dried basil.
2. Mix well.

Sweet Spice Mix (USA)

This is great for pumpkin pie, gingerbread, or baked apples.

¼ cup nutmeg
2 TB. grated ginger
2 TB. allspice berries
2 TB. cardamom seed
1 tsp. black pepper
1 tsp. whole clove
3 cinnamon sticks

1. In a small bowl, combine nutmeg, ginger, allspice berries, cardamom seed, black pepper, whole clove, and cinnamon sticks.

2. Grind to a fine powder using a coffee grinder.

Za'atar (Middle East)

This blend is popular in Lebanon, Turkey, Jordon, Syria, and North Africa. It's commonly mixed with olive oil and used as a dip for bread or a marinade for olives.

¼ cup sesame seed
¼ cup thyme
¼ cup sumac
1 TB. dill seed
1 TB. anise seed
1 TB. dried oregano
1 TB. kosher salt
Zest of 2 lemons

1. In a small bowl, combine sesame seed, thyme, sumac, dill seed, anise seed, dried oregano, kosher salt, and lemon zest.

2. Grind to a fine powder using a coffee grinder.

Condiments

This list provides descriptions of condiments mentioned throughout this book. It does not provide recipes, because most are long and involved. Production often includes fermentation, long reduction, or just plain nasty ingredients. But like spices and herbs, these condiments lend flavor to foods. And they're interesting, to boot!

Amazu Shoga   Japanese pickled ginger, served with sushi.

Anchoiade   A paste from Provençe made with anchovies, olive oil, garlic, capers, and herbs, used as a spread for bread and a dip for vegetables.

Bagoong   A Philippine paste made from fermented ground shrimp, used in many curries, sauces, and as a condiment.

Beni Shoga   A Japanese pickled ginger, colored red by *perilla* leaf. It's commonly served with fried noodles and Gyūdon (beef bowl), a popular fast food that consists of a bowl of rice topped with savory beef and onions.

Bitters   A spirit distilled from aromatic herbs, bark, roots, seeds, and citrus. It is used to flavor *aperitifs* and cocktails.

Cassareep   A bitter sugar syrup from the West Indies made from cassava juice, brown sugar, and spices. It's commonly used in a Caribbean stew called pepper pot.

Fish Sauce   A condiment made from fermented raw or dried fish. There are many versions around the world made from specific fish and according to specific techniques. Many recipes include other flavorings, including spices and herbs. Although it may smell fishy, the fish flavor cooks away, adding a rich, deep flavor to recipes.

Garum   An ancient Roman fish sauce made from fish innards, vinegar, spices, and wine, Garum was considered an aphrodisiac, and as such was reserved for the upper class. It's still produced in Spain and is favored as an alternative to salt, as it contains taste-enhancing glutamates.

Gremolata   An Italian condiment made from chopped lemon zest, parsley, garlic, and sometimes anchovies. It's the classic accompaniment to the braised veal dish Osso Bucco.

Harissa Sauce   A Tunisian hot paste made from chiles, garlic, cumin, coriander, caraway, and olive oil. It's an important ingredient in North Africa and a typical accompaniment to couscous.

Hoisin   A sweet Chinese sauce made from fermented soybeans, garlic, vinegar, sweet potato, and chiles used as a recipe ingredient, barbecue sauce, and as a condiment.

Kecap Manis   A thick soy sauce from Indonesia flavored with star anise, garlic, and palm sugar. It's used in recipes as a replacement for traditional soy sauce and as a dipping sauce.

Kochu Chang/Gocgujang   A Korean chile bean paste made from fermented soybeans, dried chiles, and garlic used to marinate meat, stews, and *bibimbah*, a popular dish of rice covered with vegetables, meat, and an egg.

Mirin   A Japanese rice wine used as a recipe ingredient and condiment.

Miso   There are many varieties of this paste made from fermented soybeans injected with a fungus derived from rice, barley, or soybeans. After aging, the result is salty, sweet, and earthy. It's used to flavor broth, sauces, dressing, dips, and as a condiment.

Nam Pla   A fish sauce from Thailand, usually made from anchovies.

Natto   A popular breakfast food in Japan made from steamed, fermented soybeans, mashed into a sticky, cheeselike consistency, and commonly eaten on top of rice.

Nuoc Mam   A fish sauce from Vietnam made from anchovies and other small fish.

Persillade   A French combination of equal parts chopped garlic and parsley. *Persil* is the French word for "parsley."

Ponzu   A Japanese sauce made from mirin, rice vinegar, *konbu*, and dried flaked tuna (*katsuobushi*). It's used as a dip, marinade, and condiment.

Preserved Lemons   A North African condiment, in which lemons are sliced open and packed in salt. As they age, the salt mixes with the acidic lemon juice and softens the lemons. Sometimes spices are added, including red pepper, coriander, clove, cinnamon, and bay.

Rakkyo   A type of Japanese shallot, usually pickled in vinegar.

Sambal   A condiment made from chile peppers, sugar, and salt. There are many variations, including those from Malaysia, Indonesia, Sri Lanka, and Singapore. Some contain other ingredients such as garlic, tomato, amchoor, kaffir lime, shrimp paste, and tamarind.

Shottsuru   A fish sauce from Japan made from the sandfish.

Sofrito   A Latin American condiment used widely in Cuban cuisine. There are many variations, but most include garlic, onions, chile peppers, and cilantro.

Tabasco   A small red pepper from the Mexican state of Tabasco, grown in Louisiana specifically for use in the pepper sauce of the same name. The McIlhenny company of Avery Island, Louisiana, combines the chiles with vinegar and salt, and ages the blend in white oak barrels for 3 years.

Tahini   A Middle Eastern paste made from sesame seeds and used as a condiment and in recipes such as hummus and halva. A similar Japanese version is called *neri-goma*.

Chile Pepper Guide

Chile peppers can be intimidating. Not only are they hot, but there are a lot of them, and they often look alike. In this appendix, I give you some basic chile pepper information to help you navigate through spicy recipes, as well as the chile pepper section of your market.

Commonly Used Fresh and Dried Chiles

There's no standard method of naming chiles. They could be named for a guy, a town, or a characteristic of their appearance or flavor. And if that weren't confusing enough, chiles have aliases. They can have different names in different parts of the country and even different names when fresh or dried.

One common bond among chile peppers is that they all contain *capsicum*, the compound that creates the sensation of heat on the tongue. In the early 1900s, Wilbur Scoville was the first to carefully measure the amount of heat in chiles. Here's a quick breakdown of Scoville Units (SU; higher Scoville Units exist for things like police pepper spray, but you won't be cooking with that stuff, I hope!):

Temperature	Range
Mild	0 to 2,000 SU
Moderate	2,500 to 23,000 SU
Hot	12,000 to 50,000 SU
Very hot	50,000 to 325,000 SU

Scoville measured the peppers' heat by diluting chile pepper extract with sugar until the heat was no longer detectable; today, the measuring is done with more precise methods. Despite all the technology, though, the range of heat for each chile still varies tremendously. While the Scoville Unit for a cayenne chile might register 30,000 today, next week it might register 50,000 due to variations in growing conditions, including weather, soil, and neighboring crops.

Hot Stuff

Capsicum can create some discomfort, especially on tender, sensitive skin. To be safe, wear gloves when chopping chiles, and keep your hands away from your eyes. Hot stuff indeed!

Chiles, both fresh and dried, have varying availability depending on where you live. Throughout the west, they can be found in most big city markets. For the rest of the world, where you might not be able to find peppers in your market, there's always the Internet. Try melissas.com for fresh and dried chiles, or chileplants.com if you want to grow your own.

Let's get to the chiles!

Anaheim

4 to 6 inches long, tapering to a point

Available fresh

Mildly hot

Also called *California* and *Chiles Verde* when green, Anaheim chiles ripen to red, at which time they can be dried, and go by the name *California Red*, *Colorado*, or *California Chile Pods*. These are what you'll find inside a can of green chiles. They're just barely hotter than a bell pepper.

Ancho

3 to 5 inches long, triangular or heart shaped

Available dried

Mildly hot

These brown, dried Poblanos are commonly used for enchilada sauce.

California Red

4 to 6 inches long, tapering to a point

Available fresh and dried

Mildly hot

These are red Anaheims. When dried, they're often decoratively strung together.

Cascabel

1 or 2 inches round

Available dried

Very hot

You'll know this reddish-brown dried chile when you hear it. Its seeds are loose inside and can be heard when shaken, like a bell.

Cayenne

4 or 5 inches long

Available dried

Hot

These peppers ripen green to red. They're mainly seen dried and ground.

Chiles del Arbol

2 or 3 inches long, very thin

Available dried

Very hot

These bright red chiles are quite hot and are often used in sauces, oils, and vinegars. They're also known as *bird's beak chiles*.

Chipotle

2 or 3 inches long, tapering to a point

Available dried

Hot

These are jalapeño chiles that have been smoked and dried. They are available loose or canned in adobo sauce.

Colorado

6 to 8 inches long, tapered

Available fresh and dried

Mild

These are Anaheim chiles, ripened to red. They're also available dried and used as the base of Colorado sauce.

Guajillo

2 or 3 inches long, tapered to a point

Available dried

Hot

This dark orange-brown chile has a fairly smooth skin and a hot but also sweet and fruity flavor.

Habanero

2 inches long, short, and wrinkly

Available fresh

Very hot

Look out for these bright orange chiles! They're cute, but they're deadly.

Hungarian Cherry

2 inches round

Available fresh

Very hot

These can be used green, but the flavor—and heat—intensifies as the chile ripens to red.

Hungarian Yellow Wax

1 or 2 inches long, tapering to a rounded point

Available fresh

Moderately hot

If left on the vine, these chiles ripen to red. They're also called *Guero* and *banana peppers*.

Jalapeño

1 or 2 inches long, tapering to a rounded point

Available fresh

Moderately hot

The most commonly used chile, jalapeños are deep, dark green, sometimes red, and are available fresh, canned, and pickled.

Mulato

3 to 5 inches long

Available dried

Mildly hot

This deep, dark brown chile has a chocolaty flavor and is often used for mole.

New Mexico

4 to 6 inches long, curved

Available fresh and dried

Moderately hot

These chiles are green when fresh and then ripen to red. They're commonly used for chile paste and powder.

Pasilla

5 to 7 inches long, tapering to a rounded end

Available fresh and dried

Moderately hot

Also called *chilaca* when fresh and *pasilla negro* when dried, pasillas ripen to a deep green-brown.

Pequin

1/4 to 1/2 inch small ovals

Available dried

Very hot

Also called *chilepequeno* and *bird peppers*, these little red peppers are petite, but potent.

Poblano

4 inches long, tapering to a rounded end

Available fresh

Moderately hot

Poblanos ripen to dark green or brown-green and are most often used in Chiles Rellenos.

Santa Fe

4 to 6 inches long, curving to a point

Available fresh

Moderately hot

Santa Fe chiles ripen from yellow to orange and red. They're also known as *Santa Fe Grande* and *Big Jims* when they reach sizes up to 12 inches.

Scotch Bonnet

1 or 2 inches, like a squat bell pepper

Available fresh

Very hot

These bright yellow torpedoes are common in Caribbean cuisines.

Serrano

1 or 2 inches long, thin, and pointed

Available fresh

Hot

Available both green and red, serranos are often used in Asian cuisine. They're also often used as a hotter substitute for jalapeños.

Tabasco

1 to 1 1/2 inches long, very thin

Rarely seen fresh or dried

Hot

Tabasco chiles ripen from yellow to red. They're used specifically to make Tabasco sauce (see Appendix B).

Thai

1 inch long, thin

Available fresh

Very hot

Available both dark green and red, Thai chiles are smaller and hotter than serranos.

Basic Chile Preparations

The more you taste chiles, the more the variety of flavors become evident. Recipes call for specific chile blends for sauces and powders, but you can, of course, experiment. Here are a couple ways you can transform chiles in your kitchen.

Chili Paste

Dried chiles are commonly made into chili paste. Here's how to do this at home with your own peppers:

1. Toast whole chiles in a 400°F oven for 5 minutes, until they're soft and fragrant. Remove chiles from the oven and let cool. (As they cool, they should become crisp.)

2. When chiles are cool, break them open, carefully shake out all the seeds and discard them, along with the stems. Cover seeded chiles with hot water, and steep for 30 to 60 minutes.

3. Strain chiles from the steeping water and add to a blender. Purée, adding some steeping water as necessary, until a smooth purée forms.

Chili paste will hold for 2 or 3 days in the refrigerator and will freeze well for several weeks.

Chili Powder

To make your own chili powder:

1. Toast whole dried chiles in a 400°F oven for 5 minutes, until they're soft and fragrant. Remove chiles from the oven and let cool. (As they cool, they should become crisp.)

2. When chiles are cool, break them open, carefully shake out all the seeds and discard them, along with the stems.

3. Pulverize chiles in a coffee grinder to the desired consistency. Store airtight in a cool dark place.